An Analysis of

Hamid Dabashi's

Theology of Discontent
The Ideological Foundation of the Islamic Revolution in Iran

Magdalena C. Delgado
with
Bryan R. Gibson

www.macat.com
info@macat.com

Cover illustration: Etienne Gilfillan

Cataloguing in Publication Data
A catalogue record for this book is available from the British Library.
Library of Congress Cataloguing-in-Publication Data is available upon request.

ISBN 978-1-912303-21-2 (hardback)
ISBN 978-1-912127-99-3 (paperback)
ISBN 978-1-912282-09-8 (e-book)

Notice
The information in this book is designed to orientate readers of the work under analysis,
to elucidate and contextualise its key ideas and themes, and to aid in the development
of critical thinking skills. It is not meant to be used, nor should it be used, as a
substitute for original thinking or in place of original writing or research. References and
notes are provided for informational purposes and their presence does not constitute
endorsement of the information or opinions therein. This book is presented solely for
educational purposes. It is sold on the understanding that the publisher is not engaged
to provide any scholarly advice. The publisher has made every effort to ensure that
this book is accurate and up-to-date, but makes no warranties or representations with
regard to the completeness or reliability of the information it contains. The information
and the opinions provided herein are not guaranteed or warranted to produce particular
results and may not be suitable for students of every ability. The publisher shall not be
liable for any loss, damage or disruption arising from any errors or omissions, or from
the use of this book, including, but not limited to, special, incidental, consequential or
other damages caused, or alleged to have been caused, directly or indirectly, by the
information contained within.

CONTENTS

WAYS IN TO THE TEXT

Who Is Hamid Dabashi?   9

What Does *Theology of Discontent* Say?   10

Why Does *Theology of Discontent* Matter?   12

SECTION 1: INFLUENCES

Module 1: The Author and the Historical Context   15

Module 2: Academic Context   20

Module 3: The Problem   25

Module 4: The Author's Contribution   30

SECTION 2: IDEAS

Module 5: Main Ideas   35

Module 6: Secondary Ideas   39

Module 7: Achievement   44

Module 8: Place in the Author's Work   48

SECTION 3: IMPACT

Module 9: The First Responses   53

Module 10: The Evolving Debate   57

Module 11: Impact and Influence Today   61

Module 12: Where Next?   65

Glossary of Terms   70

People Mentioned in the Text   79

Works Cited   88

THE MACAT LIBRARY

The Macat Library is a series of unique academic explorations of seminal works in the humanities and social sciences – books and papers that have had a significant and widely recognised impact on their disciplines. It has been created to serve as much more than just a summary of what lies between the covers of a great book. It illuminates and explores the influences on, ideas of, and impact of that book. Our goal is to offer a learning resource that encourages critical thinking and fosters a better, deeper understanding of important ideas.

Each publication is divided into three Sections: Influences, Ideas, and Impact. Each Section has four Modules. These explore every important facet of the work, and the responses to it.

This Section-Module structure makes a Macat Library book easy to use, but it has another important feature. Because each Macat book is written to the same format, it is possible (and encouraged!) to cross-reference multiple Macat books along the same lines of inquiry or research. This allows the reader to open up interesting interdisciplinary pathways.

To further aid your reading, lists of glossary terms and people mentioned are included at the end of this book (these are indicated by an asterisk [*] throughout) – as well as a list of works cited.

Macat has worked with the University of Cambridge to identify the elements of critical thinking and understand the ways in which six different skills combine to enable effective thinking.
Three allow us to fully understand a problem; three more give us the tools to solve it. Together, these six skills make up the **PACIER** model of critical thinking. They are:

ANALYSIS – understanding how an argument is built
EVALUATION – exploring the strengths and weaknesses of an argument
INTERPRETATION – understanding issues of meaning

CREATIVE THINKING – coming up with new ideas and fresh connections
PROBLEM-SOLVING – producing strong solutions
REASONING – creating strong arguments

To find out more, visit **WWW.MACAT.COM.**

CRITICAL THINKING AND *THEOLOGY OF DISCONTENT*

Primary critical thinking skill: ANALYSIS
Secondary critical thinking skill: CREATIVE THINKING

Hamid Dabashi's 1997 work *Theology of Discontent* reveals a creative thinker capable not only of understanding how an argument is built, but also of redefining old issues in new ways. The Iranian revolution of 1978–9 was front-page news around the world, and in some ways it remains so today. Though it was an uprising against authoritarian royal rule, the work of a coalition of modernisers and Islamists, the revolution saw the birth of a new Islamic republic that seemed to reject pro-western democracy.

Dabashi wanted to analyse the real reasons for this change, while examining the ways in which Islamic ideologies contributed to the revolution and the republic that emerged from it. *Theology of Discontent* examines eight different Islamic thinkers, analysing how views that, superficially, appear to have little in common contributed to the modern Iranian belief system.

In addition to its insightful analytical dissection of the ideas of these eight thinkers, the book also showcases Dabashi's creative thinking skills. Reframing the debates about Iran's relationship with the west, the author traces the ways in which Iranian identity formed in reactive opposition to western ideas. In many ways, Dabashi suggested, Iran was trapped in a cycle of deliberately asserting its difference from the west – a process that was fundamental to the development of its own unique brand of revolutionary Islamism.

ABOUT THE AUTHOR OF THE ORIGINAL WORK

Born in Iran in 1951, **Hamid Dabashi** is a prolific Iranian American scholar, sociologist, and postcolonialist who specializes in Islamic studies, history, and culture. A passionate political activist in his youth, Dabashi studied in the United States, but went home to take part in the Iranian Revolution of 1978–9, before completing a double PhD back in America in 1984. His books have been highly praised, though his views on a number of subjects, including Israel, have polarized opinions. He is currently a professor of Iranian studies and comparative literature at Columbia University.

ABOUT THE AUTHORS OF THE ANALYSIS

Dr Magdalena C. Delgado holds a doctorate in international relations from the London School of Economics, where her research focused on the role of religion in the politics of the Middle East. She is currently a research associate at LSE.

Dr Bryan Gibson holds a PhD in International History from the London School of Economics (LSE) and was a post-doctoral research fellow at the LSE's Centre for Diplomacy and Strategy and an instructor on Middle Eastern politics in the LSE's Department of International History and the University of East Anglia's Department of Political, Social and International Studies (PSI). He is currently on the faculty of Johns Hopkins University and is the author of *Sold Out? US Foreign Policy, Iraq, the Kurds and the Cold War* (Palgrave Macmillan, 2015).

ABOUT MACAT

GREAT WORKS FOR CRITICAL THINKING

Macat is focused on making the ideas of the world's great thinkers accessible and comprehensible to everybody, everywhere, in ways that promote the development of enhanced critical thinking skills.

It works with leading academics from the world's top universities to produce new analyses that focus on the ideas and the impact of the most influential works ever written across a wide variety of academic disciplines. Each of the works that sit at the heart of its growing library is an enduring example of great thinking. But by setting them in context – and looking at the influences that shaped their authors, as well as the responses they provoked – Macat encourages readers to look at these classics and game-changers with fresh eyes. Readers learn to think, engage and challenge their ideas, rather than simply accepting them.

'Macat offers an amazing first-of-its-kind tool for interdisciplinary learning and research. Its focus on works that transformed their disciplines and its rigorous approach, drawing on the world's leading experts and educational institutions, opens up a world-class education to anyone.'

Andreas Schleicher
Director for Education and Skills, Organisation for Economic Co-operation and Development

'Macat is taking on some of the major challenges in university education … They have drawn together a strong team of active academics who are producing teaching materials that are novel in the breadth of their approach.'

Prof Lord Broers,
former Vice-Chancellor of the University of Cambridge

'The Macat vision is exceptionally exciting. It focuses upon new modes of learning which analyse and explain seminal texts which have profoundly influenced world thinking and so social and economic development. It promotes the kind of critical thinking which is essential for any society and economy.
This is the learning of the future.'

Rt Hon Charles Clarke, former UK Secretary of State for Education

'The Macat analyses provide immediate access to the critical conversation surrounding the books that have shaped their respective discipline, which will make them an invaluable resource to all of those, students and teachers, working in the field.'

Professor William Tronzo, University of California at San Diego

WAYS IN TO THE TEXT

KEY POINTS

- Hamid Dabashi is an Iranian-born, US-educated scholar, and is considered one of the key postcolonial* cultural critics of the twenty-first century. Postcolonial thinkers consider the various legacies of colonialism and imperialism.

- Dabashi's book *Theology of Discontent* shows how the Islamic ideology of the Iranian Revolution was formed through a dialectical* relationship with the West—that is, a relationship founded on arguments and counterarguments from two opposing viewpoints.

- The text is important because it gives readers the tools to understand Islamic ideology as a developing theory.

Who Is Hamid Dabashi?

Hamid Dabashi, the author of *Theology of Discontent: The Ideological Foundation of the Islamic Revolution in Iran* (1993), was born in Ahvaz, Iran in 1951 and raised by his illiterate and devoutly Islamic mother. After receiving his primary education in his hometown, Dabashi moved to the capital, Tehran, in August 1970, and was accepted into the University of Tehran. From an early age, Dabashi was a fierce Iranian nationalist and social activist. He attended secret poetry readings and read subversive materials as a student. He even returned from his studies in the United States to take part in the Iranian Revolution* of 1978–9, in which the head of state, Shah Mohammad Reza Pahlavi,* was overthrown, but afterwards Dabashi saw his democratic dreams for Iran destroyed by the new ruling theocratic* elite (a theocracy is a government founded on religious doctrine and law).

After finishing his undergraduate degree, Dabashi traveled to the United States in the mid-1970s to study, and was exposed to American cultural and political values. In 1984, he completed a dual PhD in sociology of culture and Islamic studies at the University of Pennsylvania, having written his thesis on the German sociologist Max Weber's* theory of charismatic authority,* a study of the devotion given to apparently exceptional individuals. He now has American citizenship and lives in New York City.

Dabashi is a prolific writer. He has written 18 books, edited four, and contributed chapters to numerous other volumes. He has published over 100 essays, articles, and book reviews on subjects relating to Iranian studies, Islam, world cinema, and the philosophy of art. His books and articles have been translated into more than 16 languages.[1]

What Does *Theology of Discontent* Say?

Theology of Discontent says that Iran's revolution of 1978–9 in which the head of state, Shah Mohammad Reza Pahlavi, was overthrown and replaced by Ayatollah Ruhollah Khomeini, the leader of an Islamic republic, would not have happened without the Islamic ideology developed by eight prominent Iranian Islamic thinkers in the decades prior to the revolution.

Dabashi explains the contributions these Iranian thinkers have made to the development of Iran's Islamic ideology. He argues that this ideology was formed in a dialectical conversation (through argument and counterargument) with the West. He also says it was influenced by

Iranians' perception of themselves in comparison with their perception of the West. These eight writers are: the thinker and activist Jalal Al-e Ahmad* (1923–69); the socialist Ali Shari'ati* (1933–77); the cleric and teacher Morteza Motahhari* (1919–79); the theologian Sayyid Mahmud Taleqani* (1911–79); the philosopher Allamah Sayyid Muhammad Hossein Tabataba'i* (1904–81); the academic and activist Mehdi Bazargan* (1908–95); the economist and human rights activist Abolhassan Bani-Sadr* (born 1933 and president from 1980); and the cleric Ayatollah Ruhollah Khomeini* (1902–89, Supreme Leader of post-revolution Iran). Dabashi's approach—examining the work of key Iranian thinkers who might otherwise have been ignored—was considered to be inventive.

Central to the text are three core themes: anti-Westernism,* Westoxification,* and othering* (the process by which a community or people develops a collective identity by building an imagined, negative, collective identity for another community or people—the West and Iran, for example).

Dabashi argues that Iranian anti-Westernism (an opposition to Western cultural and political models) has emerged as a result of a dialectical conversation between Islam and the West. Although Iran avoided being colonized* directly by Western powers during the colonial era (that is, it was never subject to foreign government or settled by foreigners), it was drawn into the imperial system. Since the early nineteenth century, both Britain and Russia have tried to impose their imperial influence on Iran. This has resulted in the formation of a national Iranian identity based on the need to resist foreign domination. Dabashi argues that Western involvement in Iran since World War II* heightened the desire among Iranians to resist control, first by Britain and Russia, and then gradually by America. This process culminated in the Iranian Revolution.

The second theme, Westoxification, is a concept that was first introduced by Jalal Al-e Ahmad, one of the Islamist ideologues* (outspoken adherents of an ideology) examined in the book. Westoxification is the attraction to and dependence on the West, an attraction that has damaged Iran's traditional, historical, and cultural ties to Islam and the Islamic world. The term derives its name from the intoxication or infatuation that destroys rational judgment and the ability to appreciate the dangers presented by the toxic substance—namely, the West. These dangers are what are seen as the West's "moral laxity, social injustice, secularism,* devaluation of religion, and obsession with money, all of which are fueled by capitalism."* The inevitable result of Westoxification is described as "cultural alienation."*[2]

Finally, the concept of "othering" is a central theme of *Theology of Discontent*. Othering refers to the process of pitching a collective identity (that of Islamic Iran, for example) against an imagined ideology (that of the Christian West, say). This approach—good against evil, capitalism* against communism,* and so on) is often used in international relations, where states point out the negative features of their neighbors to emphasize their own strengths.

Why Does *Theology of Discontent* Matter?

Theology of Discontent is considered a key text in the study of the Iranian Revolution, primarily because it is the first to explain the ideological origins of this groundbreaking event. The text provides the tools for understanding how Iran's revolutionary Islamic ideology emerged. By showing how this ideology has been shaped through perceptions of an Islamist East and a Christian West, Dabashi emphasizes how symbols have played an important role in the development of Iran's national identity. When the book was republished in 2006, its core content remained unchanged, though an extra introduction was added in the light of continuing events, such as 9/11* and the US-led invasions of Iraq (2003)* and Afghanistan (2001).*

Theology of Discontent is also important because it went beyond the speculative and catch-all explanations for the Iranian Revolution that had been given by the typical academic works on the subject. It suggested that an Islamic ideology developed by eight seminal Islamic thinkers influenced the revolutionary masses more than the other secular and populist ideologies that some said caused the revolution. The second edition, published in 2006, provided explanations of Islam and Islamic ideology that were an alternative to those that dominated academic and public debate at the time and which presented an essentialist* idea of an unchanging Islam (that is, an idea of Islam as something that can be explained and defined by certain essential characteristics regardless of political, cultural, or geographical context).

Moreover, the text offers an excellent model for analyzing other radical Islamist movements that triumphed in the aftermath of the protests, demonstrations, and civil wars that swept through the Arab world (particularly Tunisia and Egypt) in 2010, collectively known as the Arab Spring* (although it should be noted that in Egypt, the military has since regained control over the state and cracked down on Islamist movements).

NOTES

1   Columbia University, "Hamid Dabashi," accessed May 4, 2015, http://www.columbia.edu/cu/mesaas/faculty/directory/dabashi.html.

2   *The Oxford Dictionary of Islam*, "Westoxification," accessed April 29, 2015, http://www.oxfordislamicstudies.com/article/opr/t125/e2501

SECTION 1
INFLUENCES

MODULE 1
THE AUTHOR AND THE
HISTORICAL CONTEXT

KEY POINTS

- *Theology of Discontent* is an important text because it shows how complex the Islamic ideology was that led to the 1978–9 Iranian Revolution*—that is, the overthrow of the existing government and the installation of an Islamic government. It helps our understanding of contemporary Muslim–Western relations.

- Dabashi was born and raised in Iran, which explains his advanced understanding of the politics and literature of Iran; he is also a Western scholar.

- Both the Cold War* (a period of tension between the United States and its allies and the Soviet Union* and its allies between 1947 and 1991) and the Iranian Revolution had an impact on the writing of the *Theology of Discontent.*

The Work in its Context

Published in 1993, Hamid Dabashi's *Theology of Discontent: The Ideological Foundation of the Islamic Revolution in Iran* says that the Iranian Revolution of 1978–9 would not have happened without the contribution made by the Islamic ideology of eight prominent Iranian thinkers in the decades before the revolution. As a member of the postcolonialist* school of thought (that is, as a thinker concerned with the various cultural, political, and economic legacies of colonialism), Dabashi explores the development of Islamic ideology in Iran, arguing that it was formed in a "dialectical* conversation" with the West. In other words, it was shaped according to Iranians' perception of

> **❝** I wrote *Theology of Discontent* in the heat of a monumental event [the Islamic Revolution] in the contemporary history of my homeland. There is a spontaneity of narrative, an urgency of registering something quintessential about a sweeping social event about *Theology of Discontent* that now, a mere decade later and yet a whole different world in our discursive imagination, requires framing of a different sort. I am grateful for the opportunity to take the picture I began drawing about a quarter of a century ago and frame it in what I believe to be a more enduring perspective. **❞**
>
> Hamid Dabashi, personal website

themselves relative to their perception of the West. This argument can be applied not only to the Iranian Revolution—it also provides a way to understand Muslim–Western relations in the era following the terrorist attacks on America on September 11, 2001, widely known as "9/11."*

This text has become even more important because of the central role Iran continues to play in Middle Eastern politics. In the three decades since the Iranian Revolution, Iran has emerged as a major regional force, a military powerhouse, and champion of the Shi'a* sect of Islam (one of the two main branches of Islam). This has brought it into direct conflict with the United States, Israel, and their Arab allies, particularly the conservative states in the Persian Gulf. Iran's political importance in the region, especially in recent years, makes Dabashi's analysis of its ideological origins all the more valuable to those looking to understand the country.

Author's Life
Hamid Dabashi was born in Ahvaz, Iran in 1951 and raised by his

illiterate and devoutly Islamic mother. In 1970 he took up a place at the University of Tehran. From an early age, Dabashi was a fierce nationalist and social activist at a time when Iran was ruled by an autocratic* (that is, dictatorial) modernizer, Shah Mohammad Reza Pahlavi,* who ruthlessly suppressed any form of opposition.

After finishing his undergraduate degree in the mid-1970s, Dabashi was accepted into a doctoral program at the University of Pennsylvania. Here in 1984 he completed a dual PhD in sociology of culture and Islamic studies, having written his thesis on Max Weber's* theory of charismatic authority.* Dabashi had interrupted his studies briefly to return to Iran in July 1979 to advocate a democratic system of government and resist the imposition, following the Iranian Revolution, of an Islamic theocracy* (a government founded on religious principles).

In *Iran: A People Interrupted*, Dabashi describes attending a public debate about the proposed Iranian Constitution, when a group of "organized thugs … attacked [the] gathering, prevented any debate other than what [the Islamic revolutionary leader Ayatollah Ruhollah] Khomeini* had sanctioned, and brutalized people who dared to do otherwise."[1] This anecdote shows Dabashi's deep opposition to Iran's Islamist government, and also makes clear his motivation for writing *Theology of Discontent*. After completing his PhD, Dabashi secured a post-doctoral fellowship at Harvard University and then, in 1988, a teaching post at Columbia University, where he continues to be a Professor of Iranian Studies and Comparative Literature.

Author's Background

Dabashi's thinking was influenced by two factors: the Cold War and the 1978–9 Iranian Revolution. Since the 1940s, Iran played a central role in the Cold War, which pitted the United States against the Soviet Union in a geopolitical* competition for influence. After World War II,* the Soviet Union refused to withdraw its troops from Iran and urged the country's Azerbaijani and Kurdish citizens to declare independence. Iran took the matter, now known as the Azerbaijan Crisis,* to the United Nations, which condemned the Soviet Union's actions and forced it to withdraw. This was the first major confrontation between the two superpowers.*

Iran became a key Cold War battleground in the early 1950s. Britain and the Soviet Union had long competed for influence in Iran, but following the British and Soviet occupation of Iran during World War II, nationalist feelings ran high in the country, and its popular prime minister, Mohammad Mossadeq,* nationalized* Iran's British-owned oil industry (that is, he took it from private ownership by the British on behalf of the state). In the crisis that followed, the United States overthrew Mossadeq's government in 1953 and built up the Shah as an absolute monarch*—a king with supreme governmental authority. From 1953 to 1979, the Shah ruled Iran with an iron fist and tried to transform his country from a deeply religious backwater into a modern, regional powerhouse aligned with the West. These Western interventions in Iran contributed to its increasingly anti-Western Islamic ideology.

In the 1960s, the Shah began a modernization program known as the White Revolution.* This was intended to industrialize the country, break the religious authorities' hold on education, give women the right to vote, and hand back land to the poor. The Shah's efforts to modernize Iran, however, coincided with his increasingly authoritarian rule, where any protest or opposition was put down aggressively. In 1978 police officials opened fire on a crowd during a protest and set off a cycle of violence known as the Iranian Revolution that culminated in the Shah fleeing the country in January 1979. The Islamic Republic* was established soon after.

The 1978–9 Iranian Revolution had a powerful influence on Dabashi. Still a young man, he returned to Iran and argued for the establishment of a representative democracy. But such a view was unpopular with the hard-line religious authorities, which imposed a theocratic form of government and violently suppressed all opposition. The experience had a profound impact on Dabashi's outlook and influenced the writing of *Theology of Discontent*.

NOTES

1   Hamid Dabashi, *Iran: A People Interrupted* (New York: The New Press, 2007), 165.

MODULE 2
ACADEMIC CONTEXT

KEY POINTS

- The field of international relations is primarily concerned with understanding and predicting state action.
- Before the Iranian Revolution* and the establishment of an Islamic government, religion was not thought to be important in international relations. Its importance in this field has increased since the 9/11 terrorist attacks.
- Dabashi insists that Islamic ideology and its importance for international relations must be seen in terms of a Muslim–Western relationship that spans centuries.

The Work in its Context

Hamid Dabashi's *Theology of Discontent* sits within the academic fields of postcolonial studies,* international relations, and Iranian studies.

Dabashi comes from a tradition of scholars who are involved in a prominent debate about the nature of Western scholarship concerning the developing world. This academic discipline, known as postcolonial studies, aims to analyze, explain, and develop a response to the legacy of colonialism* and imperialism.* It examines the long-term consequences of situations where one country has controlled another, especially in cases where the native populations were exploited economically and denied their own forms of rule. A key focus of postcolonial studies is the politics of knowledge (concerning how ideas are created, used, and spread). Postcolonial scholars see this as being influenced by the knowledge the colonizing* nation had about the people it controlled and the dialectical* relationship (a relationship founded on opposites such as white/black or good/evil, for example)

> ❝ [I disagree with] recent scholars who, excited
> by the spectacular events of 9/11,* have been quite
> cavalier in their thoughts and very much in a hurry
> to make grandiloquent remarks about 'Islam and the
> West,' irrespective of the historical provenance of this
> categorical invention. [I] find their hurried enthusiasm
> wanting in detail, see things quite differently than they
> do, and wish, with all due respect, to state my case here
> in some analytical detail. ❞
>
> Hamid Dabashi, *Theology of Discontent: The Ideological Foundation of the Islamic Revolution in Iran*

that developed between the colonizer and the colonized. Dabashi, like other postcolonial scholars, tends to focus heavily on literature.

In *Theology of Discontent,* Dabashi tries to engage students and academics of international relations who produced analyses of the 1978–9 Islamic Revolution in Iran and its impact on foreign affairs. In particular, Dabashi challenges scholars, such as the historian Bernard Lewis* and the international relations theorist Samuel Huntington,* who he believes have portrayed Islam as a historical movement that is opposed to the culture and politics of the Western world.

Finally, Dabashi's text falls within the broad field of Iranian studies, which includes the history, politics, art, literature, and culture of Iran.

Overview of the Field

Given Dabashi's focus on eight Iranian Islamic thinkers and his central argument—that Iran's Islamic ideology was the outcome of a dialectical conversation between "the West" and "Islam"—it is clear that *Theology of Discontent* is situated mainly within the field of postcolonial studies.

This field first emerged in the early 1960s and was developed further in the 1970s. It has been shaped by thinkers such as the French psychiatrist and theorist Frantz Fanon,* the philosopher Jean-Paul Sartre,* and the cultural critic Edward Said,* who have all written extensively and critically about imperialism*—the policy and practice of empire building—and decolonization* (the process, significant in the period from 1946 to 1975, by which a nation claims its independence).

The first notable study of postcolonialism was Fanon's famous text *Wretched of the Earth*, which criticized the dehumanizing effects of colonial rule and called for decolonization.[1] Sartre then applied the ideas to his book on France's colonial wars in North Africa, *Colonialism and Neocolonialism*.[2] Both books set the stage for a method of critical analysis highlighting the continuing effects of colonialism in Western literature.

In 1979, the Palestinian American thinker Edward Said developed the ideas further in his famous critique of Western scholarship, *Orientalism*. In this text, Said said that all Western study of the Middle East was not only biased but completely incapable of objective scholarship. He was particularly angry that Western scholars portrayed Arab and Islamic culture as backward and trapped between "tradition"* and "modernity."*[3] His work firmly established postcolonial studies as a legitimate field of academic inquiry.

Academic Influences

Hamid Dabashi says in the introduction and conclusion of *Theology of Discontent* that the book's main influences are the German social philosopher Jurgen Habermas,* the American anthropologist Clifford Geertz,* the Hungarian sociologist Karl Mannheim,* and the German sociologist Max Weber.* Of these, Weber's influence is perhaps the most obvious. Dabashi's doctoral thesis (co-authored with the sociologist Philip Rieff)* applied Weber's theory of charismatic authority*—an analysis of the way leadership is conferred on remarkable ("charismatic") individuals—to the Prophet Muhammad* (the founder of the Islamic faith); Dabashi argued that the Prophet was a charismatic leader, capable of cultivating a wide range of followers.

Weber's influence is also evident in Dabashi's first book, *Authority in Islam*, which was published in 1989. In it, he used the theory of charismatic authority to analyze the responses of three major Islamic sects (Sunni,* Shi'a,* and Khariji*) to the transformation of the Prophet Muhammad's* authority and the prophetic movement itself.[4]

The influence of Weber, Geertz, and Mannheim on *Theology of Discontent* is clear in the way Dabashi highlights the role of symbolism*—the use of symbols to represent things such as concepts or qualities—within discussion. This is an idea that is common to the works of all of these influential scholars. For example, in *Theology of Discontent* Dabashi writes that "the rhetoric of the symbolics fought at ideological and utopian* battle lines is much more compelling and immediate than the bricks and mortar of domestic and foreign affairs."[5] "Utopia" here refers to a perfect society that almost certainly does not exist.

Dabashi's work is also heavily influenced by postcolonial scholars such as Fanon, Sartre, and particularly Said. Dabashi was a junior colleague of Said at Columbia University, and shared his deep interest in the politics of the Islamic world and the Third World (that is, the developing world). In particular, Dabashi was drawn to Said's critique of patronizing Western attitudes towards Middle Eastern, Asian, and North African societies. The influence of postcolonial scholarship is evident throughout *Theology of Discontent*.

NOTES

1 Frantz Fanon, *Wretched of the Earth*, trans. Richard Philcox (New York: Grove Press, 2005).

2   Jean-Paul Sartre, *Colonialism and Neocolonialism*, trans. Azzedine Haddour (London: Routledge Classics, 2006).

3   Edward Said, *Orientalism* (London: Penguin Books, 1978).

4   Hamid Dabashi, *Authority in Islam* (New Brunswick, NJ: Transaction, 1989).

5   Hamid Dabashi, *Theology of Discontent* (Piscataway, NJ: Transaction Publishers, 2006), 25.

THE PROBLEM

KEY POINTS

- The main question of Dabashi's *Theology of Discontent* is "what caused the Iranian Revolution* of 1978–9?"
- There is no general agreement as to the causes of Iran's revolution, though scholars have begun to focus on ideology, economics, and politics.
- Dabashi explained the revolution by focusing on the works of eight ideologues* who helped shape Iran's Islamist ideology.

Core Question

When Hamid Dabashi first published *Theology of Discontent* in 1993, the main debate among scholars of Iran was about the origins of the 1978–9 Iranian Revolution. The revolution caught scholars, analysts, politicians, and even most Iranians completely off guard. At the time, no one imagined that a strong leader like the Shah, Mohammad Reza Pahlavi,* could fall and be replaced by a religious government so rapidly. This has led to decades of scholarship on the question of how his regime collapsed.

There is a wide range of literature examining the factors contributing to the development of Iran's revolutionary spirit. This includes analyses not only of the revolution's leader, Ayatollah Ruhollah Khomeini,* but also of what the Islamic take-over of Iran might mean in the context of the Cold War* (the decades-long standoff between the Soviet Union* and the United States and their aligned nations) and international affairs in general. Much of that scholarship in the immediate aftermath of the revolution was speculative, and continued to be so for some years.

> ❝ [The] daily columns in national [American] and
> international media, print, and television and the
> avalanche of propaganda pamphleteering encircling
> them all are entirely beyond hope and repair. ❞
>
> Hamid Dabashi, *Theology of Discontent: The Ideological Foundation of the Islamic Revolution in Iran*

Theology of Discontent offered an alternative to the mainstream speculation about the cause of the revolution: Iran's development of a revolutionary Islamic ideology. Dabashi argues that Iran's Islamic ideology was developed in the works of eight important Iranian Islamic ideologues, whose works he analyzes in detail in the text.

The Participants

The main debate that Dabashi addresses in *Theology of Discontent* is the ideological roots of the 1978–9 Iranian Revolution, though Islam itself is also analyzed. The historiography* (the study of the writing of history) of the revolution falls into three categories: journalistic accounts published immediately after the revolution; primary sources published by people who participated in the events; and scholarly accounts, such as Dabashi's. By the time Dabashi published his text, there were at least 50 different books, and over a hundred articles, dealing with various aspects of the Iranian Revolution.[1] Only the most seminal (that is, influential and groundbreaking) texts will be discussed here.

In the late 1980s, a number of English language scholars published accounts of the revolution based on news reports and personal experience.[2] The best of these is the American scholar James A. Bill's* *The Eagle and the Lion*, which drew on his many years of living in Iran, and his experience consulting with the US government. He was one of the first to suggest that the Shah's regime was on the brink of collapse in 1978, but he was ignored. His text has since become the intellectual foundation for modern studies of the revolution and also of US–Iran relations.[3]

Other scholarship in the late 1980s focused on the role ideology* played in bringing about the revolution.

In 1988, the sociologist Saïd Amir Arjormand* published *The Turban for the Crown* and the author Mohammad Salehi* published *Insurgency through Culture and Religion*. Both books examined the role that ideology, culture, and class played in the revolution and the period afterwards. There are, however, important differences between the two texts. Like Dabashi, Arjormand focuses on intellectual history, examining the vast amount of literature Iran produced in the years prior to the revolution, and engaging in theoretical debates about the nature of revolution itself.[4] Salehi, however, deals with ideology in more general terms. This is perhaps why one reviewer described his text as a "cursory attempt to explain the Iranian revolution to an undifferentiated 'American audience.'"[5] Clearly, in the period prior to the publication of *Theology of Discontent* scholars were already engaged in a debate over the role ideology played in bringing about the Iranian Revolution.

The Contemporary Debate

In the decades since Dabashi published *Theology of Discontent*, many scholars have entered the debate about the origins of the Iranian Revolution. A year after *Theology of Discontent* was first published, Mohsen M. Milani,* a political and international affairs analyst, published *The Making of Iran's Islamic Revolution*, which attempted to analyze factional politics in Islamic Iran. At the turn of the millennium, Seyed Sadegh Haghighat* published *Six Theories about the Islamic Revolution's Victory*, which presented a number of important views on the root causes of the Islamic Revolution of Iran. Of all the recent publications, this text is the closest to mirroring Dabashi's analysis in

Theology of Discontent.

The most recent major text on the Iranian Revolution is the British political commentator Michael Axworthy's* detailed study of the revolution and its aftermath, *Revolutionary Iran*, which combines an examination of the ideological roots of the revolution with an up-to-date political history of Iran. Significantly, this text provides one of the most accessible accounts of Ayatollah Khomeini's ideological development and how it contributed to the philosophy of the revolution.[6]

There is also a further group of studies that deals with the Iranian Revolution—namely, the various biographies of Ayatollah Khomeini. The Iranian writer Amir Taheri's* *The Spirit of Allah: Khomeini and the Islamic Revolution* (1986) and the journalist Baqer Moin's* *Khomeini: Sign of God* (1999) both examine Khomeini's role in the revolution by examining his personal experiences and how they shaped his world view and ideology.

Dabashi's text deals with complex issues and covers territory that is largely unfamiliar to non-experts; before starting it, students are advised to read Axworthy's *Revolutionary Iran*. Axworthy's text is not only highly accessible, it also provides its readers with the tools needed to fully understand *Theology of Discontent*.

NOTES

1 See Charles Kurzman, "Historiography of the Iranian Revolutionary Movement," *Iranian Studies* 28, 1–2 (1995): 25–38.

2 For a list of the best texts on the revolution, see Kurzman, "Historiography," 36–8.

3 James A. Bill, *The Eagle and the Lion* (New Haven, CT: Yale University Press, 1989).

4 Saïd Amir Arjomand, *The Turban for the Crown* (London: Oxford University Press, 1988).

5 Mohammad M. Salehi, *Insurgency through Culture and Religion* (New York: Praeger, 1988); and Farideh Farhi, "Review: *The Turban for the Crown:*

The Islamic Revolution in Iran by Saïd Amir Arjomand; *Insurgency Through Culture and Religion: The Islamic Revolution of Iran* by Mohammad M. Salehi," *Social Forces* 68, no. 3 (1990): 944–6.

6   Michael Axworthy, *Revolutionary Iran* (London: Allen Lane, 2013).

MODULE 4
THE AUTHOR'S CONTRIBUTION

KEY POINTS

- The Islamic ideology of the Iranian Revolution* can only be understood as the result of a centuries-long encounter between Islam and the West.

- *Theology of Discontent* brought depth to academic and policy debates that viewed Islam and the Muslim world as essentialist* constructs—that is, as unchanging in their essence and to be always understood as the same regardless of context.

- Dabashi has been particularly influenced by the German sociologist and philosopher Max Weber and, like him, believes symbolism* plays an important role in debate.

Author's Aims

Hamid Dabashi wrote *Theology of Discontent* to simplify "the access of a larger community of readers to the revolutionary ideas of the most important ideologues* of the Islamic Revolution."[1] Dabashi felt there was a lack of scholarship in the West on the ideas of the revolutionary ideologues who helped develop Iran's Islamic ideology.* He was convinced that interpreters and non-specialists needed a better command of these men's ideas in order to inform their readers about why Iran acts the way it does.

Dabashi examines the work of the following eight ideologues who all contributed to the development of Iran's Islamic ideology: the thinker and activist Jalal Al-e Ahmad* (1923–69); the socialist Ali Shari'ati* (1933–77); the cleric and teacher Morteza Motahhari* (1919–79); the theologian Sayyid Mahmud Taleqani* (1911–79); the philosopher

> **❝** The rhetoric of the symbolics fought at ideological and utopian* battle lines is much more compelling and immediate than the bricks and mortar of domestic and foreign affairs. **❞**
>
> Hamid Dabashi, *Theology of Discontent: The Ideological Foundation of the Islamic Revolution in Iran*

Allamah Sayyid Muhammad Hossein Tabataba'i* (1904–81); the academic and activist Mehdi Bazargan* (1908–95, Iran's first president); the economist and human rights activist Abolhassan Bani-Sadr* (born 1933 and president from 1980); and the cleric Ayatollah Ruhollah Khomeini* (1902–89, Supreme Leader of post-revolution Iran).

This approach was inventive, and without it these thinkers might otherwise have been ignored. Most studies of the Iranian Revolution, for example, refer to Bazargan and Bani-Sadr simply in terms of their political roles in the revolution: Bazargan was the first prime minister of Iran, while Bani-Sadr was Iran's first president. Dabashi's text is unique in giving these figures a voice and credit for having helped Iran develop its Islamic ideology.

Approach

In order to explain the origins of Iran's Islamist ideology, Dabashi focuses on the notion that symbols are important. By investigating the writings of the Islamic Revolution's eight key ideologues, Dabashi shows how symbols that relate to Islam (particularly the branch of Islam known as Shi'ism*) were used in such a way that they eventually created an entirely new Islamic ideology, which he believes drove the revolution. This is an entirely novel approach to the study of the revolution, as it avoids the political narrative that most studies adopt.

Key to Dabashi's argument is the idea that Iran's revolutionary ideology developed as a by-product of an ongoing dialectical* conversation between the West and Islam. He says that Iran's revolutionary Islamic identity was formed as a construct (that is, as a theoretical concept) that pitted "the West" and its accomplices (for example, the Pahlavi dynasty,* of which the deposed Shah was a member) against Iranians, who for centuries have fought against internal and external control. Given the dual nature of this development, Dabashi places great emphasis on how these scholars have used the process of othering* to develop Iran's national ideology of resistance.

As a result of his focus on how these eight thinkers used othering to formulate Iran's ideology, Dabashi has been described as "one of the foremost exponents today of postcolonial* critical theory, whose work deserves to be called postcolonial with all the multivalence [that is, the many values] of this description."[2]

Contribution in Context

Although Dabashi's work draws heavily on the postcolonial school of thought, which is concerned with matters relating to the legacies of colonialism,* *Theology of Discontent* is an entirely original study. Dabashi's strength lies in his broad knowledge of Iranian history, politics, and literature. Indeed, no other scholar in the English-speaking world is as familiar with Iranian literature as Dabashi. This has allowed him to apply the postcolonial cultural critic Edward Said's* method of literary criticism to the works of the eight Iranian ideologues, and to place their work in the context of other ideological developments inside Iran prior to the revolution.

Postcolonialists are critical of Western study of the so-called Orient (Asia and the Middle East) because, as Said argues, it falsely represents Eastern culture as being subordinate to the West, and reinforces colonial and imperial* ideas. In *Theology of Discontent*, Dabashi praises the work of Said, who, he says, has "persuasively demonstrated [that the Orientalist* language] is … essentialist and power-basing."[3]

However, although Dabashi owes a debt of gratitude to Said for establishing a clear intellectual framework, his study is wholly original.

In its focus on postcolonial literary criticism, Dabashi's text differs from the typical English-language studies of Iran. Most studies of Iran concentrate on political developments. Among these are the British political commentator Michael Axworthy's* *Revolutionary Iran*,[4] which examined the Iranian Revolution* and its aftermath, and biographies of key historical characters, such as the scholar Abbas Milani's* *The Shah*.[5]

Although both of these texts are brilliant in their own right, they were never intended to be studies of Iran's literary evolution. Axworthy and Milani come from a different area of Iranian studies from Dabashi, who is a scholar of postcolonialism and looks at the *writing* of key individuals and how they contributed to Iran's national ideology. Nevertheless, all of these texts must be seen as part of the broader category of Iranian studies.

NOTES

1   Hamid Dabashi, *Theology of Discontent* (Piscataway: Transaction Publishers, 2006), 1.

2   "Hamid Dabashi," accessed September 15, 2012, http://www. hamiddabashi.com/.

3   Dabashi, *Theology of Discontent*, xi.

4   Michael Axworthy, *Revolutionary Iran* (London: Allen Lane, 2013).

5   Abbas Milani, *The Shah* (New York: Palgrave Macmillan, 2012).

SECTION 2
IDEAS

MODULE 5
MAIN IDEAS

KEY POINTS

- Anti-Westernism,* "Westoxification,"* and "othering"* are interlinked themes that have shaped Iran's Islamic ideology.
- Iran's Islamic ideology has been shaped by dialectical* relations between the West and Islam.
- The argument is supported with detail: the ideas of eight Islamic ideologues are meticulously surveyed.

Key Themes

The main themes of Hamid Dabashi's *Theology of Discontent: The Ideological Foundation of the Islamic Revolution in Iran* are anti-Westernism, "Westoxification" (or, in its original Farsi, *Gharbzadegi*), and the concept of othering. These themes are interlinked, and together they form Dabashi's broader argument that Iran's Islamic ideology was formed over several decades, in a dialectical,* or othering, conversation with the West.

These themes are not exclusively Dabashi's; many other studies dealing with Iran and the Middle East have highlighted similar ones. What is unique about Dabashi, however, is that he uses the themes to argue that Islamic ideology is not static. He believes it is a set of ideas that is constantly changeable, depending on its relationship with a particular "other." This is because the way that symbols are used plays a key role in reinforcing the identities of both the individual and the "other."

In the original edition of *Theology of Discontent,* Dabashi develops this argument to explain the Islamic ideology of the 1978–9 Iranian

> 66 Dabashi brilliantly demonstrates that it was 'the contemporaneity of current concerns' that motivated all of the Islamic ideologues as they reacted to the 'immediacies of contemporary Muslim realities.' At a level of detail found in no other book, he shows how these ideologues reconstructed both the 'Islamic' and the 'Ideology,' concluding that the 'Islamic' was reconstructed 'from the medieval memory of its past remembrance, under which the most varied forms of secular* ("Western") claims to political salvation are to be propagated.' 99
>
> Reza Afshari, "A Critique of Dabashi's Reconstruction of Islamic Ideology as a Prerequisite for the Iranian Revolution."

Revolution* and how it developed. In the 2006 edition, Dabashi revisited his argument following the terrorist attacks on the World Trade Center in New York on September 11, 2001 (known as 9/11),* in a world in which the relationship between Muslims and the West had become increasingly hostile. In both editions, Dabashi examines the written works, diaries, speeches, and actions of eight Iranian ideologues who have contributed to developing the country's Islamic ideology.

Exploring the Ideas

Central to the development of Iran's Islamic ideology is the country's historical relationship with the West. Westoxification is a concept that was first introduced by Jalal Al-e Ahmad* (1923–69), one of the Islamist ideologues examined in the book. This concept describes the attraction to and dependence on the West that has damaged Iran's traditional, historical, and cultural ties to Islam and the Islamic world.

Westoxification is defined as "an indiscriminate borrowing from and imitation of the West, joining the twin dangers of cultural imperialism* and political domination. [It implies] a sense of intoxication or infatuation that impairs rational judgment and confers an inability to see the dangers presented by the toxic substance, that is, the West." It involves buying into what is seen as the West's "moral laxity, social injustice, secularism, devaluation of religion, and obsession with money, all of which are fueled by capitalism,*" with the inevitable result of "cultural alienation.*"[1]

Dabashi believed that Al-e Ahmad's text marked the start of a new anti-Western phase in Iran's ideological development. According to him, it combined the socialist, nationalist, and Islamist components of Iranian thinking into a "unified ideological front against both US and Soviet imperial influences in the region, and against the central role of the Pahlavi monarch in facilitating the American drive for global domination."[2]

The concept of othering is also a key theme of *Theology of Discontent*. This refers to the process of pitching a collective identity ("Islamic Iran," for example) against an imagined ideology (such as "the Christian West"). This approach (good versus evil, capitalism* versus communism,* and so on) can be identified in international relations where states point out the negative features of their neighbors in order to emphasize their own strengths.

Take, as a contemporary example, the movie *300*, which tells the story of the Battle of Thermopylae, in which a group of 300 Greek warriors fought against a vast army of Persian invaders in 480 B.C.E. In the film, the Greeks are portrayed as human heroes (the West), while the Persians (that is, Iranians) are depicted as glowing-eyed demons ("others"), bent on global domination.

These three themes combine to show how Iran has developed over time a deeply Islamic, anti-Western, and hostile nationalist ideology.

Language and Expression

The language Dabashi employs in the text of *Theology of Discontent* is sophisticated. It deals with a wide range of cultural, religious, and historical issues—namely, Iran, Islam, and the branch of Islam known as Shi'ism,* as well as the period during and after the Iranian Revolution of 1978–9.The text also discusses the Islamic and Marxist* groups that formed in the 1960s and 1970s to fight against the Shah's regime. Many of these resistance groups—such as the Marxist Mujahedeen e-Khalq*—are unique to Iran. As a result, some prior knowledge of the key issues and a basic understanding of Iranian history is recommended for those wishing to fully understand Dabashi's text.

Dabashi's writing style is extremely detailed and puts into context contemporary social, political, and religious issues. However, he often uses sophisticated language and sentence structure, which can make it difficult to understand his main argument.The text is also somewhat long, coming in at over 600 pages.[3] Inevitably, this limits the book's reach.

NOTES

1   *Oxford Dictionary of Islam*, "Westoxification," accessed April 29, 2015, http://www.oxfordislamicstudies.com/article/opr/t125/e2501.

2   Hamid Dabashi, *Iran: A People Interrupted* (New York: The New Press, 2007), 129–30.

3   Mehran Kamrava, "*Theology of Discontent: The Ideological Foundations of the Islamic Revolution in Iran* by Hamid Dabashi," *Annals of the American Academy of Political and Social Science* 534, no. 1 (1994): 185–6.

MODULE 6
SECONDARY IDEAS

KEY POINTS

- Dabashi argues that Iran's Islamic ideology was essential to the success of the Iranian Revolution.*

- *Theology of Discontent* shows how eight key ideologues — outspoken proponents of an ideology — were key to the development of Iran's national Islamic ideology.

- The text shows how these ideologues contributed to the Iranian Revolution.

Other Ideas

Hamid Dabashi's *Theology of Discontent* has been praised for its detail and the way in which it puts into context the thinking of eight key ideologues who contributed to Iran's Islamic Revolution: the thinkers, activists, theologians, and religious and political figures Jalal Al-e Ahmad,* Ali Shari'ati,* Morteza Motahhari,* Sayyid Mahmud Taleqani,* Allamah Sayyid Muhammad Hossein Tabataba'i,* Mehdi Bazargan,* Abolhassan Bani-Sadr,* and Ayatollah Ruhollah Khomeini.* Their backgrounds as well as the political and social issues of their time are examined. They are central to Dabashi's argument that Iran's Islamic ideology was formed over several decades, in a dialectical* (or othering*) conversation with the West, and each of them needs to be discussed.

In the introduction to the text, Dabashi says that the distribution and readership of the ideologues' ideas was very important. He details the likely distribution methods throughout the book. He notes: "there is no way of knowing or retrospectively ascertaining how many people actually read and responded positively to [the] writings. We can

> ❝ The 'Islamic ideology' was the quintessential pre-requisite of 'the Islamic Revolution' in Iran. Although I am not suggesting that this ideology caused the Revolution, I do submit that 'the Islamic Revolution' could not have occurred without the 'Islamic ideology.' ❞
>
> Hamid Dabashi, *Theology of Discontent: The Ideological Foundation of the Islamic Revolution in Iran*

establish only certain organizational and institutional forums ... through which these voices were publicized. That these texts were produced by the primary architects of the revolutionary movement and that they were widely disseminated in religious and professional organizations during the pre-revolutionary period are evidence enough to give them the status of having, if not caused, then occasioned the Revolution."[1]

Exploring the Ideas

Within the text, Dabashi devotes a chapter to each of the ideologues.

* Jalal Al-e Ahmad, a prominent intellectual, developed the concept of *Gharbzadegi* ("Westoxification"). This refers to the loss of Iranian cultural identity as a direct result of taking on Western norms and practices. His writings are thought to be the first crucial ones in a chain of writings that would eventually become Islamic ideology.

* Ali Shari'ati was a committed revolutionary ideologue. He contributed to Islamic ideology by providing a vision for revolution in Iran and beyond. This vision came from his revolutionary interpretation of Shi'ism.* He was often called "the Ideologue of the Islamic Revolution." His aim was to change, not interpret. Dabashi does an excellent job in capturing Shariati's key role in the formation of the Islamic ideology.

- Morteza Motahhari was a religious cleric and lecturer who was more a teacher than a writer. His primary concern was, as Dabashi notes, "to renovate and update Islam so as to make it new, make it ideologically competitive, politically forceful, and thus in full revolutionary alert should the right moment come." Dabashi shows how Motahhari played a central role in the development of Iran's Islamic ideology.

- Sayyid Mahmud Taleqani was a senior Shi'a cleric who wanted to inspire revolutionary zeal in Iran's youth. To millions of young Iranians, Taleqani was a father figure whose promise was "delivering his children from common misery."[2]

- Allamah Sayyid Muhammad Hossein Tabataba'i was a philosopher of modern Shi'a* Islam. He made clear the philosophical foundation of the Islamic ideology, and in so doing sharpened the Muslim intellectual response to competing ideologies such as Marxism.*

- Mehdi Bazargan was a religious academic who studied engineering in France in the late 1930s, and was the Islamic Republic's* first prime minister. In his writings, he tried to explain and defend Islam with reference to the "hard sciences." This message earned him support from students of physics, chemistry, and engineering. Bazargan added a crucial "scientific" dimension to Iran's Islamic ideology.

- Abolhassan Bani-Sadr was an influential Iranian politician and writer, and the Islamic Republic's first president. He tried to develop a new, creative image of his Shi'a faith, using economic models to explain Islamic ideas. This approach was popular among urban professionals, the middle classes, and the uprooted poor.

- Dabashi's final chapter examined Ayatollah Ruhollah Khomeini, a senior Shi'a cleric, who was the leader of the Iranian Revolution and later became Supreme Leader. Ayatollah Khomeini's radical form of mystic Islamism inspired the Islamic Revolution. His concept of "vilayat al-faqi"*—the rule of the supreme jurist—was key to delivering the vision of an Islamic state. It calls for a supreme leader who is able to judge whether laws comply with Islamic law.

Overlooked

Dabashi states in the opening pages of *Theology of Discontent*: "The 'Islamic ideology' was the quintessential prerequisite of 'the Islamic Revolution' in Iran. Although I am not suggesting that this ideology caused the Revolution, I do submit that 'the Islamic Revolution' could not have occurred without the 'Islamic ideology.'"[3]

Islam was an influential force driving Iran's 1978–9 revolution, but so too were competing Marxist, secular,* and populist ideologies. In the light of recent developments in the Middle East and North Africa, particularly the rise of political Islam* and the outbreak of the Arab Spring* (the popular* insurrections that spread across the Arab world in 2010), this examination of other ideologies is an aspect of the text has become all the more important and is in danger of being overlooked.

Dabashi's analysis of the development of Iran's revolutionary Islamic ideology is a valuable tool that can be used to analyze the revolutionary and Islamic dynamics of the countries that made up the Arab Spring—Tunisia, Egypt, Libya, Yemen, Bahrain, and Syria. In each of these countries, the revolutionary forces were made up of different political and social segments that united in opposition to their respective regimes. In Egypt, Tunisia, and Libya, this opposition was largely secular and democratic. But Islamist* parties—parties who subscribe to the belief that Islam offers a guide to governmental organization—soon began to dominate the post-revolutionary political environment, in a similar way to what had happened after the revolution in Iran three decades earlier.

In short, scholars of the Arab Spring should take note of Dabashi's methodology and identify the key thinkers contributing to the formation of these emerging post-revolutionary ideologies in those other countries.

NOTES

1   Hamid Dabashi, *Theology of Discontent* (Piscataway, NJ: Transaction Publishers, 2006), 2–3.

2   Dabashi, *Theology of Discontent*, 270.

3   Dabashi, *Theology of Discontent*, 7.

MODULE 7
ACHIEVEMENT

KEY POINTS

- Hamid Dabashi showed that Iran's Islamic ideology had developed through a dialectical* conversation with the West.
- The most important factor contributing to Dabashi's success was his vast knowledge of Iranian literature.
- The need for readers to already have an above-average understanding of Iranian history and politics is a limitation of the text.

Assessing the Argument

In writing *Theology of Discontent* Hamid Dabashi wanted to give "a larger community of readers [access] to the revolutionary ideas of the most important ideologues of the Islamic Revolution."[1] By examining the literature of eight important Iranian ideologues, Dabashi gives his readers a better understanding of the origins of the Iranian Revolution* than other texts, which mainly focus on historical events.

The second edition of *Theology of Discontent*, published in 2006, was even more successful at explaining the ideological roots of the Iranian Revolution. This is mainly due to the terrorist attacks of September 11, 2001 (known as "9/11")* and the application of Dabashi's text to the more recent uprisings unfolding across the Arab world that began with the Arab Spring* of 2010. While none of these events should be seen as "caused by" Islam (although that incorrect interpretation has indeed been made), the Middle East—of which Islam is a key element—has become an urgent object of study. As Islamism*—roughly, a fusion of Islamic doctrine and politics—becomes more of a mainstream ideology in the Middle East, and the

> ❝ I am not quite sure if I can say that I am pleased that my book has found this renewed significance. In fact, I am positively certain I wish it had not. ❞
>
> Hamid Dabashi, *Theology of Discontent: The Ideological Foundation of the Islamic Revolution in Iran*

relationship between the Muslim and Western worlds grows increasingly tense, the themes Dabashi explores are becoming all the more important.

Achievement in Context

When Dabashi published the first edition of *Theology of Discontent*, Iran was in the middle of a major political upheaval. Following Iran's revolution in 1978–9, the country went from crisis to crisis, all of which influenced the development of Iran's Islamic ideology and the writing of the text.

The seizure of the US embassy in Tehran in November 1979 by a group of students and the subsequent Iran hostage crisis,* in which 51 American diplomats were held hostage for 444 days, were similarly important. The event marked the elimination of pro-democracy forces in Iran and the emergence of a group of radical Islamists, who dominate the region to this day. As a young Iranian scholar living in the United States at the time, Dabashi must have been horrified by these events.

The importance of the eight-year-long Iran–Iraq War,* which began when Iran was invaded by its neighbor Iraq in September 1980, should also be noted; during the war the Iranian Islamists consolidated power, opposition to the regime was ruthlessly put down, and hundreds of thousands of young Iranians were slaughtered in combat. The war ground to a halt in August 1988, soon after the leader of the revolution and one of Dabashi's key ideologues, Ayatollah Ruhollah

Khomeini,* died of a heart attack. This triggered a power struggle that saw Ayatollah Ali Khamenei* emerge as the new supreme leader. He continued to advance Iran's revolutionary Islamic ideology, even though the moderate Akbar Hashemi Rafsanjani* became president. Rafsanjani tried to rebuild Iran's shattered economy and improve relations with the United States and the West but was unsuccessful. These domestic events had a profound impact on Dabashi's argument and the success of his text.

The second edition of *Theology of Discontent* was a product of the post-9/11 international climate. Although Dabashi recognized that his argument was still relevant, he adapted it to deal with events such as 9/11, the US "War on Terror"* that was fought across the Middle East and in parts of East Africa in response, Iran's controversial nuclear program,* and the warlike attitude of its president, Mahmoud Ahmadinejad,* who was elected in July 2005.[2] From Dabashi's perspective, these developments reinforced the relevance of the arguments he was making in *Theology of Discontent*.

Limitations

As its title indicates, *Theology of Discontent: The Ideological Foundation of the Islamic Revolution in Iran* deals with a specific cultural, religious, and historical context—that of Islam, Shi'ism,* and the Islamic Revolution of 1978–9. Although Dabashi provides a well-rounded analysis of the issues at hand, readers do need to have at least some understanding of the background. And because the book was written about a specific historical event, a general understanding of the Iranian Revolution and the historical forces that led to it is also required.

The key themes of *Theology of Discontent*—anti-Westernism,* Westoxification,* and othering*—are, however, of universal value. Of these, the most important is the concept of othering—the process of creating a collective identity (in this case, "Islamic Iran") through opposition to an imagined ideology (here, the "Christian West").

Another key argument that continues to be relevant is the idea that the Islamic ideology behind the revolution was the result of a dialectical conversation between Islam and the West. From this perspective, Islam, and its ideology, is fluid and constantly remaking itself, but the direction it takes will be decided by who or what Islam is in conversation with.

As far as *Theology of Discontent* is concerned, the "conversation partner" was the West (the Pahlavi dynasty* of Shah Mohammad Reza Pahlavi was seen as an extension of the West, and so falls into that category) or the Soviet Union.* This key idea can be applied beyond *Theology of Discontent.* It can explain the creation of ideologies unconnected to the Islamic Revolution and to Islam. It can also aid the study of Islam and Muslim–Western relations in a post-9/11 world.

In the introduction to the book's second edition, Dabashi emphasizes this latter point—one of the main reasons for its re-publication in 2006.

NOTES

1   Dabashi, *Theology of Discontent* (Piscataway, NJ: Transaction Publishers, 2006), 1.

2   Elissa Gootman, "Security Council Approves Sanctions against Iran Over Nuclear Program," *New York Times*, December 24, 2006.

MODULE 8
PLACE IN THE AUTHOR'S WORK

KEY POINTS

- Hamid Dabashi has written widely about Islam, Shi'ism,* Iran, and Muslim–Western relations, from a postcolonial* perspective.

- *Theology of Discontent* was Dabashi's first major publication; its themes are visible throughout the rest of his work.

- Hamid Dabashi is regarded as one of the leading scholars of postcolonial* critical theory.

Positioning

Theology of Discontent was not Hamid Dabashi's first book; that was *Authority in Islam* (1989), a work that set the stage for his career. In it, he applied the German sociologist Max Weber's* concept of charismatic authority* to the responses of three major Islamic sects (Sunni,* Shi'a, and Khariji*) to the authority of the Prophet Muhammad* and the prophetic movement.[1]

While writing this first book he developed the central ideas of *Theology of Discontent*. He also developed his postcolonial style, exploring the relationship between philosophy, literature, and the politics of resistance, and using Iran as a case study.[2] When he first published *Theology of Discontent*, Dabashi was still a young scholar, not yet established as a mainstream academic.

Theology of Discontent was Dabashi's first major publication. In the introduction to the second edition of the text, published in 2006, he writes that he had spent decades researching its content and that it contained ideas that he had formulated at the beginning of his career.

> **❝** Hamid Dabashi is one of the foremost exponents today of postcolonial critical theory, whose work deserves to be called postcolonial with all the multivalence [many values] of this description. In his work, postcoloniality does not mean a denial or denunciation of the modern European tradition of philosophy and social theory, but their effortless absorption into a larger, more complex reflection. **❞**
>
> Sudipta Kaviraj, "The World is My Home"

Integration

Dabashi's early books include *History of Islamic Philosophy* (1996), *Truth and Narrative: The Untimely Thoughts of 'Ayn al-Qudat* (1999), and *Staging a Revolution: The Art of Persuasion in the Islamic Republic of Iran* (2002).[3]

His works can be divided into two categories: those that deal with the politics of resistance, such as *Theology of Discontent*; and the texts that focus on art and film.

The vast majority of his work focuses on the politics of resistance, where he often uses Iran as a case study. With the exception of *Authority in Islam*, most of his work was published after *Theology of Discontent*. This text established a postcolonial method of analysis of the politics of resistance that he continues to use to this day.

Theology of Discontent is still a model for Dabashi's more recent publications. This is especially evident in his books *Iran: A People Interrupted* (2007), about the relationship between Iran's intellectual heritage and the development of its anti-colonial* ideology,*[4] and *Post Orientalism: Knowledge and Power in Time of Terror* (2008),[5] which applies the concepts of anti-Westernism, Westoxification,* and othering* to the War on Terror.*

Dabashi's interest in decolonization* and the politics of resistance is also evident in *Islamic Liberation Theology: Resisting the Empire* (2008), *Iran, The Green Movement and the USA: The Fox and the Paradox* (2010), *Shi'ism: A Religion of Protest* (2011), *The Arab Spring: The End of Postcolonialism* (2012), and *Corpus Anarchicum: Political Protest, Suicidal Violence, and the Making of the Post-Human Body* (2012).[6]

Theology of Discontent established a workable framework of analysis that Dabashi still uses in publications dealing with Iran and its revolutionary ideology. It also shows Dabashi's deep interest in explaining Iran's intellectual development to the West.

Dabashi's second area of intellectual interest is Iranian art and cinema. He has published several texts, including *Close Up: Iranian Cinema, Past, Present, Future* (2001) and *Masters & Masterpieces of Iranian Cinema* (2007).[7] He sits on the juries of a number of international film festivals, and advises film producers.[8]

Significance

Theology of Discontent is Dabashi's most popular publication. According to Google Scholar, it has been cited in over 250 different publications. By comparison, his 2012 text *The Arab Spring* has been cited 131 times, and *Iran: A People Interrupted* has been cited 94 times. His book on Iranian cinema, *Close Up*, has been cited 114 times.

Theology of Discontent lies within the field of postcolonial studies, but it has not become one of its leading texts. Other postcolonial scholars are cited far more often. For example, Frantz Fanon's* *The Wretched of this Earth* has been cited over 10,000 times, Jean–Paul Sartre's* *Being and Nothingness* over 7,000 times, and Edward Said's* *Orientalism* over 1,500 times. Nevertheless, it would be unfair to criticize a modern text for not being as popular as the scholarship that formed the basis of an entire field of study. Moreover, the very purpose of subsequent scholarship is to support, modify, or refute previous work. To this end, Dabashi was entirely successful at applying the model first established by Fanon, Sartre, and Said to Iran, particularly in the linking of literature and art to politics.

NOTES

1 Hamid Dabashi, *Authority in Islam* (New Brunswick, NJ: Transaction, 1989).

2 Hamid Dabashi, in *History of Islamic Philosophy*, eds. Seyyed Hossein Nasr and Oliver Leaman (London: Routledge, 1996); Hamid Dabashi, *Truth and Narrative: The Untimely Thoughts of 'Ayn al-Qudat al-Hamadhani* (London: Curzon Press, 1999); Hamid Dabashi, *Theology of Discontent* (Piscataway, NJ: Transaction Publishers, 2006); Hamid Dabashi and Peter Chelkowski, *Staging a Revolution: The Art of Persuasion in the Islamic Republic of Iran* (New York: New York University Press, 2002).

3 Hamid Dabashi, *History of Islamic Philosophy* (Abingdon: Taylor & Francis, 1996); Dabashi, *Truth and Narrative*; Dabashi and Chelkowski, *Staging a Revolution*; and Dabashi, *Theology of Discontent*.

4 Hamid Dabashi, *Iran: A People Interrupted* (New York: The New Press, 2007).

5 Dabashi, *Theology of Discontent*.

6 Hamid Dabashi, *Islamic Liberation Theology: Resisting the Empire* (London: Routledge, 2009); Hamid Dabashi, *Iran, The Green Movement and the USA: The Fox and the Paradox* (London: Zed Books, 2010); Hamid Dabashi, *Shi'ism: A Religion of Protest* (Cambridge, MA: Belknap Press, 2011); Hamid Dabashi, *The Arab Spring: The End of Postcolonialism* (London: Zed Books, 2012); and Hamid Dabashi, *Corpus Anarchicum: Political Protest, Suicidal Violence, and the Making of the Post-Human Body* (New York: Palgrave-MacMillan, 2012).

7 Hamid Dabashi, *Close Up: Iranian Cinema, Past, Present, Future* (London: Verso Publishers, 2001); and Hamid Dabashi, *Masters & Masterpieces of Iranian Cinema* (Washington, DC: Mage Publishers, 2007).

8 For details about Dabashi's involvement in film, see his website: www. HamidDabashi.com/cinema-and-art/.

SECTION 3
IMPACT

MODULE 9
THE FIRST RESPONSES

KEY POINTS

- *Theology of Discontent* was initially criticized for offering little more than a historical narrative of eight important twentieth-century Iranian thinkers.

- Dabashi responded to the historical limitations of *Theology of Discontent* by publishing a second edition of the book in which he expands on its ideas.

- The terrorist attacks against the United States on September 11, 2001 ("9/11")* created a need to draw wider conclusions about the "Islamic ideology."* This shaped the reception of the second edition.

Criticism

The response to Hamid Dabashi's *Theology of Discontent* has been mixed. The most common criticism is that Dabashi exaggerated the impact the eight ideologues* had on the 1978–9 Iranian Revolution.* The sociologist Misagh Parsa,* for example, suggests that "as an analysis of the connection between ideology and revolution, the book is a failure." He argues that Dabashi does not provide enough proof to back up his argument.[1]

Another critic, the historian Reza Afshari,* recalls that the popular Iranian recording artists Sousan* and Aghasi* were the "real cultural phenomena of the time" and that they were far more effective in reaching and mobilizing people than Dabashi's ideologues.[2] The implication is that Dabashi's beliefs about how the Islamic ideology developed led him to present his material in a way that served his own narrative.

> ❝ I am grateful for the opportunity to take the picture I began drawing about a quarter of a century ago and frame it in what I believe to be a more enduring perspective—perhaps a permanently changed worldview. ❞
>
> Hamid Dabashi, *Theology of Discontent: The Ideological Foundation of the Islamic Revolution in Iran*

However, one important scholar on Iran, Ervand Abrahamian,* disputes this. He points out that *Theology of Discontent* did not "pretend to be a comprehensive analysis of the causes, course, and outcome of the Iranian Revolution, or a path-breaking comparison with other revolutions—including obscure ones in ancient Greece."[3] Indeed, Dabashi writes in his introduction that his book is limited to an examination of the "revolutionary ideas of the most important ideologues of the Islamic Revolution," and stresses that this "Islamic ideology [did] not explain the whole story; it merely sets the 'discourse' and the 'universe' in which the revolution unfolded."[4] As Mehran Kamrava* notes, "The deceptively simple task that the book sets for itself, the reconstruction of the Islamic ideology, is one of its greatest strengths. Dabashi refrains from such lofty attempts as, for example, placing the Iranian Revolution within a broader Shi'ite or Islamic framework or exploring the social and political causes of the revolution. Such tasks each require separate books in themselves."[5]

Even in the opening pages of *Theology of Discontent,* Dabashi points out that he is not suggesting that these eight scholars alone caused the revolution; they were simply the "primary architects of the revolutionary movement" in Iran, and the fact that their writings had been "widely disseminated in religious and professional organizations during the pre-revolutionary period [is] evidence enough to give them the status of having, if not caused, then occasioned the Revolution."[6]

Responses

After *Theology of Discontent* was first published in 1993, Dabashi did not join his critics in a public debate. When the second edition came out in 2006, however, he included a new introduction. Here, he tried to "remedy [the original edition's] historical limitations by expanding on its thematic and theoretical propositions."[7] Dabashi indicated that he "wanted to take the picture [he] began drawing about a quarter of a century ago and frame it in what [he] believe[s] to be a more enduring perspective—perhaps a permanently changed worldview."[8] This suggests that he wanted to place the new version in the context of the world as it had become following the terrorist attacks on the twin towers of the World Trade Center on 9/11, feeling that the arguments he had originally put forward in the early 1990s were still relevant.

Dabashi offers another motive for publishing the second edition: "Much that has happened in world history warrants reconsideration of my argument and the evidence I put forward in some considerable detail."[9] It is clear from his new introduction that Dabashi was deeply affected by the terrorist attacks against the United States on September 11, 2001, which made "what he had to say then, far more critically significant now."[10]

Conflict and Consensus

In the time between the first and second publication of *Theology of Discontent*, Dabashi's views seem to have deepened. In the new edition, he emphasizes his original argument about the formation of Islamic ideology; his understanding of the relationship between East and West is now presented in the context of a post-9/11 world, where perceptions of East and West have been aggravated by a growing process of othering.* Putting forward such an informed understanding, Dabashi argues, will lead to a more accurate analysis of the Western–Muslim relationship.

The change in the international climate that occurred in the 13 years between the two editions was enormous, especially with respect to Iran. Dabashi's text offers his readers insight into a side of Iran that few people actually understand. As the renowned historian of the Middle East Gertrude Bell* noted in 1891, Iranian social and political life was "a life into which no European can penetrate."[11]

James A. Bill,* a leading American expert on Iran, shares this sentiment, writing, "The Iranian social and political process is extremely difficult to penetrate, understand, and explain."[12] *Theology of Discontent* exposed Western readers to the ideological frame of mind that drove Iran's Islamic Revolution and that has dominated its political system ever since. It is a profoundly important text for those who want to understand Iran.

NOTES

1   Misagh Parsa, "Ideology and Revolution in Iran," *Middle East Report* 25, no. 5 (1995): 31.

2   Reza Afshari, "A Critique of Dabashi's Reconstruction of Islamic Ideology as a Prerequisite for the Iranian Revolution," *Critique* 3, no. 5 (1994): 65.

3   Ervand Abahramian, "Review: *Theology of Discontent* by Hamid Dabashi," *International Journal of Middle East Studies* 28, no. 2 (1996): 299.

4   Hamid Dabashi, *Theology of Discontent* (Piscataway, NJ: Transaction Publishers, 2006), 1.

5   Mehran Kamrava, "Review: *Theology of Discontent* by Hamid Dabashi," *Annals of the American Academy* 534, no. 1 (1994): 186.

6   Dabashi, *Theology of Discontent*, 2–3.

7   Dabashi, *Theology of Discontent*, x.

8   Dabashi, *Theology of Discontent*, ix.

9   Dabashi, *Theology of Discontent*, ix.

10 Dabashi, *Theology of Discontent*, ix.

11 Gertrude Bell, *Persian Pictures*, 3rd ed. (London: Ernest Benn, 1947), 31.

12 James A. Bill, *The Eagle and the Lion* (New Haven, CT: Yale University Press, 1989), 10.

MODULE 10
THE EVOLVING DEBATE

KEY POINTS

- As with Dabashi's other works, *Theology of Discontent* has made clear the complexities of Iran's Islamic ideology.*

- This ideology is built on the ever-changing interactions between Muslims and the West, a dialectical* conversation that has been taking place for centuries.

- As a stand-alone text, *Theology of Discontent* has had no direct impact on international relations; but it has advanced the view that "Islamic ideology" results from a dialectical Muslim–Western relationship.

Uses and Problems

Since the original publication of *Theology of Discontent* in 1993, Hamid Dabashi has developed his ideas in several subsequent publications—namely, *Iran: A People Interrupted* (2007), *Islamic Liberation Theology* (2008), and *Shi'ism: A Religion of Protest* (2011). Each of these texts examines similar themes through a skillful analysis of Iran's literary and intellectual development.

Iran: A People Interrupted is the most direct application of the methodology first employed in *Theology of Discontent*. Dabashi examines 200 years of Iranian literature, poetry, and politics to show how Iran's dominant ideology—what he calls an anti-colonial* modernity*—evolved naturally through the interaction between, on the one hand, Iranian intellectuals, politicians, writers, and poets, and on the other, Enlightenment* ideals, such as democracy* and civil disobedience.*[1]

Today, Iran continues to be relevant in terms of Middle Eastern

> ❝ [It] is no more valid to speak of Islam, and certainly not of political Islam, as some kind of monolith with a fixed anti-western viewpoint, than it would be to ignore the immense cultural, linguistic and religious diversity of the west, and to claim that it is, or has become, an anti-Islamic force bent on subjugating Muslims. ❞
>
> Gary Brown, "Mutual Misperceptions"

politics. Sectarian* debates within Islam have deepened since the US-led invasion of Iraq in 2003* and the establishment there of a government dominated by Shi'ites.* A fiercely anti-Western* sentiment has grown, despite cooperation between Iran and the West over the rise of the militant Islamist* organization Islamic State of Iraq and Syria* (ISIS). For this reason, *Theology of Discontent* remains relevant, and a third edition of the text would be a welcome addition to the growing debate over Iran's role in the region.

Schools of Thought

Within the field of postcolonial* literary criticism there is widespread admiration for Hamid Dabashi's work. Vanessa Martin,* a professor of Middle Eastern history at Royal Holloway, University of London, commends Dabashi for "bringing out rich aspects of Iranian culture that are little known or not recognized."[2] The intellectual historian Susan Buck-Morss* hailed his work for being "exemplary of a new Leftist discourse that is undogmatic and non-sectarian … open and intimate."[3] Gayatri Spivak,* a fellow postcolonial critic, a disciple of Edward Said,* and one of Dabashi's colleagues at Columbia, felt that Dabashi had taken on the difficult task of writing a "history of Iran that teaches us how to understand a people overshadowed by the grand narratives of political (mis)representation."[4]

Theology of Discontent deals with many themes while developing a critical literary approach to the study of Islam, Iran, Muslim–Western relations, and postcolonialism. The impact of Dabashi's work can be appreciated by looking at the different fields of study in which those praising it have been involved, from scholars of Middle Eastern and Iranian history, to postcolonial literary and artistic critiques.

Nevertheless, there is no way to decide whether a school of thought has emerged around *Theology of Discontent*. The success of Dabashi's work is shadowed by that of his mentor, Edward Said, whose text *Orientalism* continues to lead the field of postcolonial studies. Significantly, with the death of Said in 2003, this field has broadened beyond its original concern with orientalist views of the Middle East. This is especially true in the United Kingdom, where the Postcolonial Studies Association has encouraged students to take up this field of study and widen the scope of its scholarship.[5] However, despite such expansion, there is still no evidence of a single group of scholars who identify exclusively with Dabashi's work.

In Current Scholarship

Hamid Dabashi is respected across a range of academic fields, most notably in Middle Eastern studies, Iranian history, postcolonial literary criticism, and international relations. His standing is not just due to the success of *Theology of Discontent,* although this text is Dabashi's most frequently cited work. Rather, his reputation in these fields has grown in line with his publications and the development of his career. This is because his works deal consistently with the same themes and theoretical areas: Islam, Iran, and Muslim–Western relations seen through a postcolonial lens.

Although "disciples" may be too big a term to use for them, there are several scholars from these fields who agree with the ideas Dabashi puts forward in *Theology of Discontent*. In international relations, for example, one prominent scholar, the Lebanese American international relations professor Fawaz Gerges,* has echoed Dabashi's argument that many academics and politicians view Islam as an essentialist,* violent religion, and that it deserves a broader understanding. Fred Halliday,* an important scholar of Middle Eastern studies and international relations, agreed, noting that the Middle East is widely misunderstood, despite having contributed significantly to Western history. After all, Christianity—the dominant religion in the West—originated in the Middle East.[6] Roger Owen* and Talal Asad* are two other leading scholars writing in the field of Middle Eastern studies and history who also agree with Dabashi's argument.[7]

Despite the shared ground between these scholars and Dabashi, they cannot be seen as his disciples because most of them were already active prior to the publication of *Theology of Discontent* and none point to Dabashi's work as being a source of inspiration.

However, since they all express a very similar message in their academic work (as well as in mainstream media), they can be considered to comprise an intellectual movement.

NOTES

1   Hamid Dabashi, *Iran: A People Interrupted* (New York: The New Press, 2007).

2   Vanessa Martin, "Review of Hamid Dabashi's *Iran: A People Interrupted*," *Middle East Journal* 61, no. 4 (2007): 719.

3   Hamid Dabashi, "Advance Praise for *Iran: A People Interrupted*," official website of Hamid Dabashi, accessed September 25, 2013, http://www.hamiddabashi.com/iran-a-people-interrupted/.

4   *The New Press*, "*Iran: A People Interrupted* by Hamid Dabashi," accessed September 25, 2013.

5   Postcolonial Studies Association, "Members," accessed June 18, 2014, http://www.postcolonialstudiesassociation.co.uk/members/.

6   See Fred Halliday, *Arabia without Sultans* (London: Saqi Books, 2002).

7   See Roger Owen, *State, Power and Politics in the Making of the Modern Middle East* (New York: Routledge, 2004); and Talal Asad, *Formations of the Secular: Christianity, Islam, Modernity* (Stanford: Stanford University Press, 2003).

IMPACT AND INFLUENCE TODAY

KEY POINTS

- *Theology of Discontent* is seen as a key work in the tradition of postcolonial* literary criticism.

- Some critics have suggested that Dabashi's writing is actually anti-modernist,* although it is not the case that he is opposed to modernity.*

- Dabashi and sympathetic scholars say that the "Islamic ideology"* must be examined in the light of a historically complex dialectic* between Muslims and the West.

Position

Hamid Dabashi's *Theology of Discontent* addresses the question of Iran as a significant force in global affairs. Geographically, the country is in a perfect place for political strategy: it occupies the eastern shore of the Persian Gulf, controlling access to the Strait of Hormuz, a narrow waterway through which roughly 32 percent of the world's oil supply passes.[1] With a highly educated population of over 80 million people, Iran sits on the fourth largest oil reserves and the third largest natural gas reserves in the world. It is a major regional economic powerhouse. More importantly, those who follow the Shi'a* sect of Islam tend to look to Iran for spiritual guidance. This has put it at odds with Saudi Arabia, which is seen as the regional champion of the Sunni* faith. Iran is also involved in a range of sectarian* military conflicts (wars between different Islamic sects) in the aftermath of the Iraq War* and the Arab Spring.*

Although the work is important in terms of the explanation it offers of Iran's behavior, and despite all of the factors that make *Theology*

> ❝ Hamid Dabashi's writings on Iranian culture and politics brilliantly re-imagine the rich heritage of a shared past and a conflicted present. His reflections on revolution and nationhood, poetry and cinema, philosophy and the sacred, are urgent, provocative, complex, and highly original. ❞
>
> Timothy Mitchell, "The World is My Home"

of Discontent relevant to contemporary debates about Iran, there is no evidence that it has had a broader influence among academics or Iran experts. This does not mean that the text is irrelevant—simply that it has not had enough attention to play a role in the debate.

Interaction

Theology of Discontent and Dabashi's later works cut across the fields of postcolonial studies, Middle Eastern studies, and international relations. They also enter deeply into the debate about the origins of the Iranian Revolution.* Dabashi follows in Edward Said's* footsteps and criticizes Orientalist* scholarship, which portrays Arab and Islamic culture as backward and takes a patronizing view of Middle Eastern, Asian, and North African societies.

In the introduction to the 2006 edition, Dabashi suggested that after 9/11* scholars produced rushed analyses that made pompous and flawed statements about the West's relationship with Islam. Dabashi attacks those whom he views as the main culprits: Bernard Lewis,* Samuel Huntington,* Kenneth Pollack,* and the neoconservatives* in the administration of President George W. Bush* (people who subscribed to the belief, very roughly, that the Western economic and democratic model should be defended and promoted through military means), who all proposed interventionist* policies in the Middle East, particularly in Iran.

Many publications in recent years have examined the origins of the Islamic Revolution of Iran.

In 1994, a year after *Theology of Discontent* was published, the scholar Mohsen M. Milani* published *The Making of Iran's Islamic Revolution: From Monarchy to Islamic Republic.* This presents an analysis of factional politics in Islamic Iran. In 2000, Seyed Sadegh Haghighat published *Six Theories about the Islamic Revolution's Victory*. This collected a number of important views on the root causes of Iran's revolution. Other scholars have looked to economic explanations. The energy analyst and journalist Andrew Scott Cooper's* *The Oil Kings*, for example, argues that a Saudi decision to lower oil prices in late 1976 sent Iran's economy into a tailspin. This in turn led to social unrest and then revolution.[2] More recently, the political commentator Michael Axworthy* published his detailed study *Revolutionary Iran* (2013), which combined an examination of the ideological roots of the revolution with a political history of Iran after the revolution.[3]

Some scholars have taken a more biographical approach. The Iranian-born writer Amir Taheri's* *The Spirit of Allah: Khomeini and the Islamic Revolution* (1986) and the BBC* journalist Baqer Moin's* *Khomeini: Sign of God* (1999), for instance, focus on the revolution's leader, Ayatollah Ruhollah Khomeini.*

The Continuing Debate

The first edition of *Theology of Discontent* was written to explain the ideological roots behind Iran's 1978–9 Islamic Revolution. The second edition, published in 2006, was a response to the contempt that marked public debate on Islam and Muslim–Western relations after 9/11 and the US-led invasions of Afghanistan in 2001* and Iraq in 2003.*

Indeed, the debate that was taking place generally was an excellent example of the process of othering:* Islam was presented in terms of violence, terrorism, intolerance, and bigotry, while the West was seen as calm, peaceful, and tolerant. In the second edition, Dabashi criticized two scholars in particular—Gilles Kepel* and Olivier Roy*—who both played a prominent role in debates about Islam and the Middle East and their relationship with the West after 9/11. Dabashi describes Kepel's book *War for Muslim Minds: Islam and the West* as "the most compelling confusion of modern Islamic political thought to have emerged in the post-9/11 *marché folklorique* of neo-Orientalism." And he accuses Roy of ignoring the "extraordinary role that 'Islamic ideology' (or what he calls 'Islamist Ideology') has played over the last two centuries in resisting systematic colonial incursions into Muslim lands."[4]

Despite these criticisms, Kepel and Roy never engaged in a public debate with Dabashi. It is difficult therefore to know whether Dabashi's challenge to these "rushed analysts" affected their thinking or approaches to studying the region. Judging from recent publications from both scholars, it seems his views were not only ignored, they were not even acknowledged.

NOTES

1   Bryan R. Gibson, "Bypassing Hormuz," *The Majalla,* July 6, 2012, accessed April 30, 2015, http://eng.majalla.com/2012/07/article55232901.

2   Andrew Scott Cooper, *The Oil Kings: How the US, Iran, and Saudi Arabia Changed the Balance of Power in the Middle East* (New York: Oneworld, 2011).

3   Michael Axworthy, *Revolutionary Iran* (London: Allen Lane, 2013).

4   Hamid Dabashi, *Theology of Discontent* (Piscataway, NJ: Transaction Publishers, 2006), xxxiv.

MODULE 12
WHERE NEXT?

KEY POINTS

- *Theology of Discontent* is an important addition to those works that warn against a simplistic analysis of the complexity of Muslim–Western relations.

- As Muslim–Western relations continue to be strained, *Theology of Discontent* will provide a good reference point for understanding.

- *Theology of Discontent* is seminal because it gives readers the tools to understand the "Islamic ideology"* as something fluid and changing.

Potential

Hamid Dabashi's *Theology of Discontent* will surely continue to be a relevant text. It offers a unique insight into the 1978–9 Iranian Revolution* and the emergence of an Islamic Republic* built on a radical, spiritual, revolutionary, and aggressively anti-Western* ideology. Dabashi's second edition in 2006 placed Iran in the context of the world post-9/11,* with the waging of the War on Terror* and the US-led invasions of Afghanistan (2001)* and Iraq (2003).*

The text will be useful for scholars, journalists, diplomats, and policy makers, especially those who deal with political Islam,* Shi'ism,* the overtly patriotic ideology of nationalism,* and specific topics such as US–Iran relations, Iranian foreign policy, nuclear diplomacy (in light of Iran's nuclear program*), and revolutions.

Dabashi's text will also continue to be important for as long as Western journalists, academics, and policy makers portray the West's relationship with Islam as a confrontation between "us" and "them." It

> **❝** Because of [Theology of Discontent] it will be harder for scholars sympathetic to the Islamists to repeat with credulity current clichés as the Muslims' rejection of 'Western' secularism,* Muslim authenticity and anticolonialist reassertions of Islamic culture. **❞**
>
> Reza Afshari, "A critique of Dabashi's Reconstruction of Islamic Ideology as a Prerequisite for the Iranian Revolution"

contributes to the continuing postcolonial* debate about Edward Said's* critique of Orientalist* scholarship of the Middle East and Islam, which he saw as biased and incapable of being objective. The topics Dabashi engaged with in 1993—the politics of resistance, ideology, imperialism,* power, and control—are just as relevant today as they were then.

Future Directions

Dabashi is respected across a range of academic fields. He has managed to position Iran and Middle Eastern topics within emerging academic disciplines while linking them to topical social and historical events. As a result, there are several scholars in Middle Eastern Studies, Iranian history, postcolonial literary theory, and international relations who share Dabashi's concerns about the portrayal of Islam in the West. In the field of international relations, the Lebanese-American academic Fawaz Gerges* echoes Dabashi's distaste for the way Islam has been portrayed as an essentialist* and inherently violent religion, agreeing with his belief that Islam should be studied in context.

Fred Halliday,* a prominent scholar of Middle Eastern studies and international relations who died in 2010, argued, like Dabashi, that the Middle East, especially the Arab Middle East, was poorly understood, despite having the longest history of contact with the West.[1] Roger Owen* and Talal Asad*—both prominent scholars in the field of

Middle Eastern studies and history—supported this argument.[2] These scholars, however, cannot be considered disciples of Dabashi, as they are influential in their own right and were active long before him.

Summary

At the heart of *Theology of Discontent* is Dabashi's view that Iran's revolution in 1978–9 would not have happened without the formation of an Islamic ideology developed by eight important Iranian Islamic thinkers in the decades beforehand. Dabashi details the contributions that these thinkers made to the development of Islamic ideology in Iran. But he has a broader argument: Iran's Islamic ideology was formed in a "dialectical* conversation" with the West, and it was shaped according to Iranians' perception of themselves and of the West. Symbols were used to reinforce both their own identity and that of the West as they perceived it.

This argument has proved useful outside the context of the Iranian Revolution, providing a way in which one can understand Muslim–Western relations in the post-9/11* world.

Theology of Discontent is seminal for many reasons, most notably for the timelessness of the book's underlying argument. The text gives readers the tools for a more general understanding of Islamic ideology, beyond its historical context and its Iranian setting. It presents Islamic ideology as something changeable, shaped by an individual's sense of an "other," with symbols being used to reinforce both the individual's identity and that of the other. The book's re-publication in 2006 with just an additional introduction to put the argument in context proves its timelessness.

Other factors, too, show the importance of *Theology of Discontent*. The book offered a specific interpretation of the cause of the Iranian Revolution, claiming that it happened because of the Islamic ideology developed by eight prominent Iranian Islamic thinkers in the decades beforehand.

Dabashi has been commended even by his critics[3] for the level of detail and context he gives to social, political, and cultural issues. In this respect, the book is arguably unmatched in any of the academic fields to which it belongs. *Theology of Discontent* is an important text. It is valuable and unique—even if the perception of its importance is to some extent reliant on the eminent status of its author as a leading expert on issues relating to Iran, Islam, and associated areas.

NOTES

1   See Fred Halliday, *Arabia without Sultans* (London: Saqi Books, 2002).

2   See Roger Owen, *State, Power and Politics in the Making of the Modern Middle East* (New York: Routledge, 2004); and Talal Asad, *Formations of the Secular: Christianity, Islam, Modernity* (Stanford: Stanford University Press, 2003).

3   See Afshari, Reza, "A Critique of Dabashi's Reconstruction of Islamic ideology as a Prerequisite for the Iranian Revolution," *Critique: Critical Middle Eastern Studies* 3, no. 5 (1994): 67.

GLOSSARY

GLOSSARY OF TERMS

Absolute monarchy: a form of government where a monarch has unchecked power to rule their land as they see fit.

Afghanistan War (2001–): refers to the military intervention by North Atlantic Treaty Organization (NATO) and Allied Forces following the September 11 attacks on America.

Anti-colonialism: opposition to control by one country over another, generally for the purpose of economic exploitation.

Anti-modernism: an ideology that opposes modernity and all of the things associated with it.

Anti-Westernism: opposition to or hostility toward the interests of European and North American nations.

Arab Spring: a term used to describe a series of violent and non-violent protests, demonstrations, and civil wars that swept through the Arab world in 2010. As a result of the Arab Spring, rulers have been forced from power in Tunisia, Egypt, Libya, and Yemen, and civil wars have erupted and are continuing in Bahrain and Syria.

Autocracy: a system of government in which one person has absolute power.

Azerbaijan Crisis (1946–7): a Cold War* crisis that occurred following World War II, when the Soviet Union refused to withdraw its troops from Iran and then urged Iran's Azerbaijani and Kurdish citizens to declare independence. Iran took the matter to the United

Nations, which condemned the Soviet Union's actions and forced it to withdraw.

BBC: the British Broadcasting Corporation.

Capitalism: an economic system in which privately owned goods and services are exchanged for profit.

Charismatic authority: a concept developed by the sociologist Max Weber* that explains people's complete devotion to the exceptional heroism or exemplary character of an individual person, and the patterns they portray.

Civil disobedience: the conscious refusal to follow unjust laws on the basis that it is more just to break unjust laws than to obey them. It is used as a peaceful form of political protest.

Cold War (1947–91): period of tension between the United States and the Soviet Union which avoided direct military conflict, but was conducted through espionage and proxy wars.

Colonialism: control by one country over another, generally for the purpose of economic exploitation.

Colonized: see Colonialism.

Communism: an economic system originally proposed by Karl Marx in which the means of production are collectively owned. Marx envisioned a communist society as having no social classes.

Cultural alienation: To be isolated from a group on the basis of your culture.

Cultural imperialism: the cultural aspects of imperialism. In its modern form, it involves the exportation of culture from the developed to the developing world; throughout the developing world, for example, people drink Coke and wear Mickey Mouse T-shirts.

Decolonization: the process of a nation ridding itself of colonial influence, which marked the period between 1946 and 1975, when many nations claimed their independence.

Democracy: system of government where all the eligible members of a state participate equally in the election of representatives through regular elections.

Dialectical: process of arriving at the truth, or a coherent synthesis, by combining two opposing statements or viewpoints. This process is particularly associated with the work of the German philosopher Friedrich Hegel.

Enlightenment: a Europe-wide intellectual movement that arose in the late seventeenth century. It put reason, rather than superstition or religion, at the heart of all human endeavors.

Essentialism: a view that certain properties are essential to any particular entity and that this entity is definable by those properties.

Geopolitical: a term used to describe a form of politics influenced heavily by geographical factors.

Historiography: the study of the writing of history.

Ideologue: an outspoken adherent of an ideology.

Ideology: a branch of knowledge concerned with the origin and nature of ideas.

Imperialism: policy of extending a country's power and influence over other countries through the use of diplomacy or military force.

Intervention: refers to any concerted and state-led effort by one country to determine the political direction of another country.

Iran hostage crisis (1979–81): on November 4, 1979, a group of students who claimed to be acting on behalf of Ayatollah Khomeini seized the US embassy in Tehran and held 51 American diplomats hostage for 444 days. This led to a break in US–Iran relations that has continued to this day.

Iranian Revolution (1978–9): a popular uprising in Iran that saw the overthrow of the Pahlavi dynasty and the Shah, Mohammad Reza Pahlavi, and the establishment of an Islamic Republic, under the Ayatollah Ruhollah Khomeini.

Iran–Iraq War (1980–1988): major military conflict between Iran and Iraq. It began when Iraq invaded Iran in September 1980 and came to an end in 1988, when Iraq won a decisive victory.

Iran's nuclear program: since the early 1990s, Western powers have accused Iran of developing nuclear weapons. The Iranian government has maintained a right to develop peaceful nuclear technology and has denied a nuclear weapons program. Negotiations about the issue have taken place periodically since 2003.

Iraq War (2003–11): armed conflict between the United States and Iraq. After toppling the government of Saddam Hussein in 2003, the conflict descended into a sectarian civil war, which pitted Iraq's Shi'a and Sunni populations against each other. In December 2011, American forces withdrew from Iraq.

Islamic Republic of Iran: formed in 1980 in the aftermath of the Iranian Revolution. It is a theocracy, led by a supreme jurist who ensures that all legislation abides by Islamic law.

Islamic State of Iraq and Syria* (ISIS): a militant, and notoriously brutal, Islamist organization active across the borders of Iraq and Syria and governing territory there.

Islamism: refers to a range of ideologies that view Islam as a source of social and political guidance.

Khariji: a group of Muslims who initially supported the Shi'a following the prophet Muhammad's death but later turned against the Imam Ali. They insisted that any Muslim could be a leader of the Muslim community and had the right to revolt against any ruler who deviated from their interpretation of Islam.

Marxism: doctrine originating from the views of the economist and social theorist Karl Marx (1818–83) and, to a lesser extent, the industrialist Friedrich Engels (1820–95), who highlighted the class struggle inherent in capitalist societies, and argued for communal ownership of the state in order that social divisions be eliminated.

Modernity: relates to the modern era, where traditional or feudal values have been replaced by enlightened values.

Mujahedeen e-Khalq: Iranian Marxist terrorist group that was founded in 1965 in opposition to the Shah's regime. Even since the

1978–9 Iranian Revolution, the group has continued to fight for the overthrow of the government.

Nationalism: a belief, creed, or political ideology that involves individuals identifying with, or becoming attached to, their nation.

Nationalization: the transfer of a branch of industry or commerce from private ownership to the state. For example, imagine a government seizing control of all the oil companies in its country.

Neoconservatism: an American political movement that emphasizes proactive promotion of free markets and the aggressive promotion of democracy via military force.

9/11: the name given to a series of terrorist attacks on New York City and Washington, DC on September 11, 2001. The attacks, orchestrated by the militant Islamist group Al Qaeda, killed around three thousand people.

Orientalism: concept referring to the general patronizing nature of Western attitudes towards Middle Eastern, Asian, and North African societies.

Othering: the process of creating a collective identity ("Islamic Iran," for instance) against an imaginative construction ("the Christian West"). This approach is often used in international relations, in situations where states point out the negative attributes of their neighbors to emphasize their own strengths.

Pahlavi dynasty: refers to the rule of Reza Shah Pahlavi (1878–1944), who became king in a coup in 1925 and was overthrown by the British and Russians in 1941, and that of his son Mohammad Reza Pahlavi (1919–80), who ruled from 1941 until his overthrow in 1979.

Political Islam: an ideology that combines the central ideals of Islam with politics.

Popular: carried out by the people.

Postcolonialism: an academic discipline established in the early 1960s that focuses on analyzing intellectual discourses between colonial powers and those whom they colonize in order to analyze, explain, and respond to the legacies of both colonialism and imperialism.

Sectarian: a term denoting or concerning a sect or sects.

Secular: non-religious, or a belief in the separation between Church and State.

Shi'ism/Shi'a/Shi'ite: one of the two main branches of Islam; it broke from the majority Sunni sect following the death of the prophet Muhammad in 632 C.E. The dominant religion inside Iran, its followers reject the first three Sunni caliphs and regard the Imam Ali, the fourth caliph, as Muhammad's first true successor.

Soviet Union, or USSR: a kind of "super state" that existed from 1922 to 1991, centered primarily on Russia and its neighbors in Eastern Europe and the northern half of Asia. It was the communist pole of the Cold War, with the United States as its main "rival."

Sunni: the most popular branch of Islam, with roughly 90 percent of Muslims identifying with this sect. It differs from Shi'ism through its acceptance of the first three caliphs, following the Prophet Muhammad's death.

Superpower: a term coined by William T. R. Fox in 1944 to describe a very powerful and influential nation; it is often used to refer to the United States and the Soviet Union during the Cold War, when these states were the two most powerful nations in the world.

Symbolism: a term referring to the symbolic meaning attributed to natural objects or facts. The symbols employed are typically carefully chosen in order to tap into the emotions of the audience.

Theocracy: a system of government in which priests rule in the name of God or a god.

Tradition: long-established custom or belief or the passing of customs or beliefs from generation to generation.

Utopia: a concept of a place or state of things in which everything is perfect.

Vilayat al-Faqi (Rule of the Supreme Jurist): concept in Shi'a jurisprudence that calls for a creation of a supreme leader who is able to interpret whether laws comply with Islamic law. The concept first gained prominence after Ayatollah Ruhollah Khomeini published a series of lectures calling for the creation of an Islamic government ruled by this principle.

War on Terror: a term often applied to the American-led military campaign against the terrorist groups involved in the terrorist attacks on the United States that took place on September 11, 2001.

Westoxification: a term that combines the words "West" and "toxic" to describe the way in which other cultures borrow and imitate the West. In particular, this concept warns against the dangers of Western cultural imperialism and political domination of the developing world.

White Revolution: a series of reforms in Iran that were launched in 1963 by the Shah, Mohammad Reza Pahlavi, and which were designed to transform Iran into a modern industrial state, while limiting the power of the Iranian aristocracy and the religious establishment.

World War II (1939–45): a global conflict fought between the Axis Powers (Germany, Italy, and Japan) and the victorious Allied Powers (United Kingdom and its colonies, the former Soviet Union, and the United States).

PEOPLE MENTIONED IN THE TEXT

Ervand Abrahamian (b. 1940) is a professor of history at City University of New York who specializes in modern Iranian history. He is notable for his work on the 1953 coup in Iran.

Reza Afshari is a professor of history at Pace University, focusing on human rights in Iran, Islamic politics, and Islamic cultural relativism.

Aghasi is the stage name for Elvin Agassi, an Assyrian-born Iranian musician who has released numerous folk records.

Jalal Al-e Ahmad (1923–69) was a prominent Iranian writer, thinker, and social and political activist. He is famous for coining the term *Gharbzadegi* (Westoxification).

Mahmoud Ahmadinejad (b. 1956) is an Iranian politician who was the sixth president of Iran from 2005 to 2013. His two terms in office were noted for the rapid expansion of Iran's nuclear program that took place and for his anti-Semitic (that is, showing hostility to Jewish people) rants.

Saïd Amir Arjormand is a professor of sociology at the State University of New York. His work focuses primarily on Iranian law and politics.

Talal Asad (b. 1933) is Distinguished Professor of Anthropology at City University of New York. His prominent works include *Thinking about Secularism and Law in Egypt* (2001) and *Formations of the Secular: Christianity, Islam, Modernity* (2003).

Michael Axworthy (b. 1962) is a British academic, author, and political commentator who served as the head of the Iran section at the British Foreign & Commonwealth Office between 1998 and 2000. He is most noted for his studies of Iranian history, notably *Revolutionary Iran* (2013) and *Empire of the Mind* (2007).

Abolhassan Bani-Sadr (b. 1933) was the first president of Iran, serving from 1980 to 1981. An economist and a human rights activist, he was impeached by the Iranian Majles (parliament) in June 1981 and fled the country.

Mehdi Bazargan (1908–95) was an academic, activist, and the first prime minister of Iran after the Iranian Revolution. He resigned in November 1979 after activists seized control of the US embassy in Tehran, taking 51 Americans hostage for 444 days.

Gertrude Bell (1868–1926) was an English writer, political officer, administrator, spy, and archaeologist. Through extensive travels, contacts, and prolific writing, she helped map out Great Britain's Middle East policy.

James A. Bill is Professor of International Studies at William & Mary University. Focusing on the Middle East, specifically Iran, he is best known for his book *The Eagle and the Lion* (1989), which recounts the history of US–Iran relations.

Susan Buck-Morss is professor of philosophy and intellectual history at Cornell University. Her work focuses primarily on dialectics.

George W. Bush (b. 1946) was the 43rd president of the United States. He served two terms, from 2001 to 2009.

Andrew Scott Cooper is an energy analyst, journalist, and the author of *The Oil Kings: How the US, Iran, and Saudi Arabia Changed the Balance of Power in the Middle East* (2011).

Frantz Fanon (1925–61) was a Martinique-born French psychiatrist, philosopher, and revolutionary who fought for the independence of Algeria in the 1960s. His text *Black Skin, White Masks* (1952) laid the intellectual foundation for the field of postcolonial studies.

Clifford Geertz (1926–2006) was a professor of anthropology at Princeton University, best known for his work in cultural anthropology. His work is particularly concerned with conceptualizing the role of symbols in cultural contexts.

Fawaz Gerges (b. 1958) is a Lebanese-born American academic and author who has published numerous books dealing with the Middle East, US foreign policy, terrorism, and the Western world's relations with Islam. He is a professor of international relations at the London School of Economics.

Jurgen Habermas (b. 1929) is a German social philosopher and leading figure of the Frankfurt School. He is noted for having developed a cultural reappraisal of Marxism and for his work on communication theory, particularly his concept of "communicative rationality"—the idea that all speech has the inherent goal of mutual understanding.

Seyed Sadegh Haghighat graduated in political thought from TM University in Tehran, and studied at the Islamic Seminaries between 1981 and 2004. Currently he is a faculty member of the department of political science at Mofid University in Qom.

Fred Halliday (1946–2010) was a professor of international relations at the London School of Economics. His prominent publications include *Nation and Religion in the Middle East* (2000), *Two Hours that Shook the World. September 11, 2001: Causes and Consequences* (2001), and *Arabia without Sultans* (2002).

Samuel Huntington (1927–2008) was a professor of international relations at Harvard University from 1963 until his death. His book *The Clash of Civilizations and the Remaking of World Order* (1996) is widely considered the most influential post–Cold War analysis of international order.

Mehran Kamrava (b. 1964) is a professor of political science and director of the Center for International and Regional Studies at Georgetown University's School of Foreign Service in Qatar. His work focuses on the Middle East.

Gilles Kepel (b. 1955) is a French professor of political science at Science Po, and a specialist on Islam and the contemporary Arab world.

Ali Khamenei (b. 1939) is the Supreme Leader of Iran, the third president of Iran, a Shi'a cleric, and an Islamist revolutionary.

Ruhollah Khomeini (1902–89) was a religious cleric. He led the Islamic Revolution of 1978–9 that led to the overthrow of the Pahlavi dynasty and became Iran's Supreme Leader, a position he held until his death in 1989.

Bernard Lewis (b. 1916) is a neoconservative British American historian, a public intellectual, a political commentator, and an Emeritus Professor of Near East Studies at Princeton University. He became a controversial figure after the late Edward Said accused him of being a "European Orientalist."

Karl Mannheim (1893–1947) was a Hungarian-born sociologist who was influential in the early twentieth century and who is viewed as one of the founding fathers of classical sociology. He is known for his notion that ideas and beliefs are rooted in larger thought systems, and for his work on the role of leadership in society.

Vanessa Martin is a professor of Middle Eastern history at Royal Holloway in London. Her research focuses on Iran's political, religious, and social development from the nineteenth to the late twentieth century.

Abbas Milani (b. 1949) is the Hamid & Christina Moghadam Director of Iranian Studies at Stanford University and a professor (by courtesy) in the Division of Stanford Global Studies. He was a founder of the Iran Democracy Project and a research fellow at the Hoover Institution. His areas of expertise are US–Iran relations and Iranian cultural, political, and security issues.

Mohsen Milani is the executive director of the Center for Strategic & Diplomatic Studies, and Professor of Politics at the University of South Florida. He is a prolific writer, with over 60 publications.

Baqer Moin is a journalist for the British Broadcasting Company (BBC) and an author. His work is focused primarily on Iran and Islam.

Mohammad Mossadeq (1892–1967) was Iran's democratically elected prime minister between 1951 and 1953, the year in which he was overthrown in a CIA-sponsored coup. He was a fierce Iranian nationalist who was dedicated to removing British influence from Iran and its control over Iran's oil resources.

Morteza Motahhari (1919–79) was an Iranian religious cleric and lecturer whose emphasis was on teaching rather than writing. His primary concern was to renovate and update Islam so as to make it new, ideologically competitive, politically forceful, and thus on full revolutionary alert should the right moment come.

Muhammad (Prophet) (570–632) was the prophet of the Muslim faith. Born in present-day Saudi Arabia, Muhammad received the first of a series of revelations in 610 that, when transcribed, became the doctrinal basis of Islam. He is viewed as the last prophet of God.

Roger Owen (b. 1935) is a professor of Middle East history at Harvard University. His prominent books include *A History of the Middle East Economies in the Twentieth Century* (1999) and *State, Power and Politics in the Making of the Modern Middle East* (2003).

Mohammad Reza Pahlavi (1919–1980) was the king (Shah) of Iran from September 1941 until he was overthrown by a popular uprising throughout 1978–9. He fled the country in February 1979 and died of cancer in 1980. He was a close ally of the United States during the Cold War.

Misagh Parsa (b. 1945) is a professor of sociology at Dartmouth College. His research focuses primarily on Iran, dictatorships, social revolutions, and the politics of resistance.

Kenneth Pollack (b. 1966), a former Central Intelligence Agency intelligence analyst, is a National Security Staff member and an expert on Middle East politics and military affairs at the Brookings Institute.

Akbar Hashemi Rafsanjani (b. 1934) is an Iranian statesman and religious leader. After playing a lead role in organizing the mass demonstrations that led to the overthrow of the Shah, Mohammad Reza Pahlavi, he entered politics and served as president of Iran from 1989 to 1997.

Philip Rieff (1922–2006) was an influential sociologist, best known for his books about Sigmund Freud's impact on society as well as about the direction of morality and Western culture.

Olivier Roy (b. 1949) is a professor at the European University Institute in Florence. His prominent publications include *The Failure of Political Islam* (1994) and *The Politics of Chaos in the Middle East* (2007).

Edward Said (1935–2003) was a Palestinian American literary theorist, critic, journalist, and pro-Palestinian activist. He is best known for his book *Orientalism* (1978), which was a critique of the generally patronizing nature of Western attitudes towards Middle Eastern, Asian, and North African societies.

Mohammad Salehi is an Iranian-born independent scholar. His work is diverse, focusing on sociology, computer sciences, and mathematics.

Jean-Paul Sartre (1905–80) was a French philosopher who was a prominent figure in the development of the existential school of philosophy. In *Being and Nothingness* (1943), he examined the concepts of phenomenology and ontology (the nature of being).

Ali Shari'ati (1933–77) was an Iranian ideologue, revolutionary, and sociologist whose work focused on the sociology of religion. He is considered one of the most prominent Iranian intellectuals of the twentieth century.

Sousan (1943–2004) was the stage name for a popular Iranian singer and songwriter (Golandam Taherkhani) in the 1960s and 1970s.

Gayatri Spivak (b. 1942) is an Indian-born professor of philosophy at Columbia University. Her work focuses on postcolonialism and literature.

Allamah Sayyid Muhammad Hossein Tabataba'i (1904–81) was an Iranian philosopher and Shi'a cleric. He is considered one of the most prominent thinkers of philosophy and contemporary Shi'a Islam.

Amir Taheri (b. 1942) is an Iranian-born writer who tends to focus on Middle Eastern issues.

Sayyid Mahmud Taleqani (1911–79) was an Iranian theologian, reformer, and advocate of democracy. A senior Shi'a cleric of Iran, he was part of a group of religious leaders which included Ayatollah Ruhollah Khomeini, who had advocated opposition to the pro-Western secularist government of the Shah, Mohammad Reza Pahlavi.

Max Weber (1864–1920) was a German sociologist and philosopher whose concept of dialectics—which points out contradictions between two objects/groups—has had a profound impact on the study of philosophy, particularly Marxism.

WORKS CITED

WORKS CITED

Abrahamian, Ervand. *Khomeinism: Essays on the Islamic Republic*. Berkeley: University of California Press, 1993.

————. "Review: *Theology of Discontent* by Hamid Dabashi." *International Journal of Middle East Studies* 28, no. 2 (1996): 299.

Afshari, Reza. "A Critique of Dabashi's Reconstruction of Islamic Ideology as a Prerequisite for the Iranian Revolution." *Critique: Critical Middle Eastern Studies* 3, no. 5 (1994): 67–83.

Arjormand, Saïd Amir. "Fundamentalism, Religious Nationalism, or Populism?" *Contemporary Sociology* 23, no. 5 (1994): 671–5.

————. *The Turban for the Crown*. London: Oxford University Press, 1988.

Asad, Talal. *Formations of the Secular: Christianity, Islam, Modernity*. Stanford: Stanford University Press, 2003.

Axworthy, Michael. *Revolutionary Iran*. London: Allen Lane, 2013.

Bell, Gertrude. *Persian Pictures*, 3rd ed. London: Ernest Benn, 1947.

Bill, James A. *The Eagle and the Lion*. New Haven, CT: Yale University Press, 1989.

Cooper, Andrew Scott. *The Oil Kings: How the US, Iran, and Saudi Arabia Changed the Balance of Power in the Middle East*. New York: Oneworld, 2011.

Dabashi, Hamid. *The Arab Spring: The End of Postcolonialism*. Zed Books, 2012.

————. *Authority in Islam*. New Brunswick, NJ: Transaction, 1989.

————. *Close Up: Iranian Cinema, Past, Present, Future*. London: Verso, 2001.

————. *Corpus Anarchicum: Political Protest, Suicidal Violence, and the Making of the Post-Human Body*. New York: Palgrave-MacMillan, 2012.

————. "Hamid Dabashi." Accessed September 15, 2012. http://www.hamiddabashi.com/.

————. *History of Islamic Philosophy*. Abingdon: Taylor & Francis, 1996.

————. *Iran, The Green Movement and the USA: The Fox and the Paradox*. London: Zed Books, 2010.

————. *Iran: A People Interrupted*. New York: The New Press, 2007.

————. *Islamic Liberation Theology: Resisting the Empire*. London: Routledge, 2009.

―――. *Masters & Masterpieces of Iranian Cinema*. Washington, DC: Mage Publishers, 2007.

―――. *Shi'ism: A Religion of Protest*. Cambridge, MA: Belknap Press, 2011.

―――. *Theology of Discontent*. New York: New York University Press, 1993.

―――. *Theology of Discontent*. Piscataway, NJ: Transaction Publishers, 2006.

―――. *Truth and Narrative: The Untimely Thoughts of 'Ayn al-Qudat al-Hamadhani*. London: Curzon Press, 1999.

Dabashi, Hamid, and Peter Chelkowski. *Staging a Revolution: The Art of Persuasion in the Islamic Republic of Iran*. New York: New York University Press, 2002.

Dalacoura, Katerina. "Middle East and the West: Misunderstandings and Stereotypes." London School of Economics Fathom Content Database. Accessed September 25, 2013. http://fathom.lse.ac.uk/Seminars/21701764/21701764_session4.html.

Fanon, Frantz. *Wretched of the Earth*. Translated by Richard Philcox. New York: Grove Press, 2005.

Farhi, Farideh. "Review: *The Turban for the Crown: The Islamic Revolution in Iran* by Said Arjomand; *Insurgency Through Culture and Religion: The Islamic Revolution of Iran* by Mohammad M. Salehi." *Social Forces* 68, no. 3 (1990): 944–6.

Gerges, Fawaz. *America and Political Islam: Clash of Cultures or Clash of Interests?* Cambridge: Cambridge University Press, 1999.

Gibson, Bryan R. "Bypassing Hormuz." *The Majalla,* July 6, 2012. Accessed April 30, 2015. http://eng.majalla.com/2012/07/article55232901.

Gootman, Elissa. "Security Council Approves Sanctions against Iran Over Nuclear Program." *New York Times*, December 24, 2006.

Haghighat, Seyed Sadegh. *Six Theories about the Islamic Revolution's Victory*. Tehran: Alhoda Publishers, 2000.

Halliday, Fred. *Arabia without Sultans*. London: Saqi Books, 1974, 2002.

Juergensmeyer, Mark. *The New Cold War? Religious Nationalism Confronts the Secular State*. London: University of California Press, 1993.

Kamrava, Mehran. "Review: *Theology of Discontent* by Hamid Dabashi." *Annals of the American Academy* 534, no. 1 (1994): 186.

Kepel, Gilles. *War for Muslim Minds: Islam and the West*. Cambridge, MA: Harvard University Press, 2004.

Kurzman, Charles. "Historiography of the Iranian Revolutionary Movement." *Iranian Studies* 28, 1–2 (1995): 25–38.

Martin, Vanessa. "Review of Hamid Dabashi's *Iran: A People Interrupted*." *Middle East Journal* 61, no. 4 (2007): 718–19.

Milani, Abbas. *The Shah*. New York: Palgrave Macmillan, 2012.

Milani, Mohsen M. *The Making of Iran's Islamic Revolution: From Monarchy to Islamic Republic*. Boulder: Westview Press, 1994.

Moin, Baqer. *Khomeini: Sign of God*. London: I. B. Tauris & Company, 1999.

Nasr, Seyyed Hossein and Oliver Leaman (eds.). *History of Islamic Philosophy*. London: Routledge, 1996.

New Press. "*Iran: A People Interrupted* by Hamid Dabashi." Accessed September 25, 2013. http://thenewpress.com/index.php?option=com_ title&task=view_title&metaproductid=1579.

Owen, Roger. *State, Power and Politics in the Making of the Modern Middle East*. New York: Routledge, 2004.

Parsa, Misagh. "Ideology and Revolution in Iran." *Middle East Report* 25, no. 5 (1995): 30–2.

Payvand Iran News. "Book Launch: *Masters & Masterpieces of Iranian Cinema*—by Hamid Dabashi." Accessed September 25, 2013. http://www.payvand.com/news/07/may/1191.html.

Program on International Policy Attitudes. "The American Public on the 9/11 Decade: A Study of American Public Opinion." Accessed September 10, 2012. http://www.brookings.edu/research/reports/2011/09/08–opinion-poll-telhami.

Roy, Olivier. *Globalized Islam: The Search for a New Ummah*. New York: Columbia University Press, 2004.

Said, Edward W. *Orientalism*. London: Penguin Books, 1978.

Salehi, Mohammad M. *Insurgency through Culture and Religion*. New York: Praeger, 1988.

Sartre, Jean-Paul. *Colonialism and Neocolonialism*. Translated by Azzedine Haddour. London: Routledge Classics, 2006.

Shaikh, Nermeen. "AsiaSource—Interview with Hamid Dabashi." Accessed September 25, 2013. http://www.campus-watch.org/article/id/716.

Taheri, Amir. *The Spirit of Allah: Khomeini and the Islamic Revolution*. Bethesda, MD: Adler & Adler Publishers, 1986.

Weber, Max. *From Max Weber: Essays in Sociology*. Edited by H. H. Gerth and C. Wright Mills. London: Routledge, 1991.

THE MACAT LIBRARY
BY DISCIPLINE

AFRICANA STUDIES

Chinua Achebe's *An Image of Africa: Racism in Conrad's Heart of Darkness*
W. E. B. Du Bois's *The Souls of Black Folk*
Zora Neale Huston's *Characteristics of Negro Expression*
Martin Luther King Jr's *Why We Can't Wait*
Toni Morrison's *Playing in the Dark: Whiteness in the American Literary Imagination*

ANTHROPOLOGY

Arjun Appadurai's *Modernity at Large: Cultural Dimensions of Globalisation*
Philippe Ariès's *Centuries of Childhood*
Franz Boas's *Race, Language and Culture*
Kim Chan & Renée Mauborgne's *Blue Ocean Strategy*
Jared Diamond's *Guns, Germs & Steel: the Fate of Human Societies*
Jared Diamond's *Collapse: How Societies Choose to Fail or Survive*
E. E. Evans-Pritchard's *Witchcraft, Oracles and Magic Among the Azande*
James Ferguson's *The Anti-Politics Machine*
Clifford Geertz's *The Interpretation of Cultures*
David Graeber's *Debt: the First 5000 Years*
Karen Ho's *Liquidated: An Ethnography of Wall Street*
Geert Hofstede's *Culture's Consequences: Comparing Values, Behaviors, Institutes and Organizations across Nations*
Claude Lévi-Strauss's *Structural Anthropology*
Jay Macleod's *Ain't No Makin' It: Aspirations and Attainment in a Low-Income Neighborhood*
Saba Mahmood's *The Politics of Piety: The Islamic Revival and the Feminist Subject*
Marcel Mauss's *The Gift*

BUSINESS

Jean Lave & Etienne Wenger's *Situated Learning*
Theodore Levitt's *Marketing Myopia*
Burton G. Malkiel's *A Random Walk Down Wall Street*
Douglas McGregor's *The Human Side of Enterprise*
Michael Porter's *Competitive Strategy: Creating and Sustaining Superior Performance*
John Kotter's *Leading Change*
C. K. Prahalad & Gary Hamel's *The Core Competence of the Corporation*

CRIMINOLOGY

Michelle Alexander's *The New Jim Crow: Mass Incarceration in the Age of Colorblindness*
Michael R. Gottfredson & Travis Hirschi's *A General Theory of Crime*
Richard Herrnstein & Charles A. Murray's *The Bell Curve: Intelligence and Class Structure in American Life*
Elizabeth Loftus's *Eyewitness Testimony*
Jay Macleod's *Ain't No Makin' It: Aspirations and Attainment in a Low-Income Neighborhood*
Philip Zimbardo's *The Lucifer Effect*

ECONOMICS

Janet Abu-Lughod's *Before European Hegemony*
Ha-Joon Chang's *Kicking Away the Ladder*
David Brion Davis's *The Problem of Slavery in the Age of Revolution*
Milton Friedman's *The Role of Monetary Policy*
Milton Friedman's *Capitalism and Freedom*
David Graeber's *Debt: the First 5000 Years*
Friedrich Hayek's *The Road to Serfdom*
Karen Ho's *Liquidated: An Ethnography of Wall Street*

John Maynard Keynes's *The General Theory of Employment, Interest and Money*
Charles P. Kindleberger's *Manias, Panics and Crashes*
Robert Lucas's *Why Doesn't Capital Flow from Rich to Poor Countries?*
Burton G. Malkiel's *A Random Walk Down Wall Street*
Thomas Robert Malthus's *An Essay on the Principle of Population*
Karl Marx's *Capital*
Thomas Piketty's *Capital in the Twenty-First Century*
Amartya Sen's *Development as Freedom*
Adam Smith's *The Wealth of Nations*
Nassim Nicholas Taleb's *The Black Swan: The Impact of the Highly Improbable*
Amos Tversky's & Daniel Kahneman's *Judgment under Uncertainty: Heuristics and Biases*
Mahbub Ul Haq's *Reflections on Human Development*
Max Weber's *The Protestant Ethic and the Spirit of Capitalism*

FEMINISM AND GENDER STUDIES

Judith Butler's *Gender Trouble*
Simone De Beauvoir's *The Second Sex*
Michel Foucault's *History of Sexuality*
Betty Friedan's *The Feminine Mystique*
Saba Mahmood's *The Politics of Piety: The Islamic Revival and the Feminist Subject*
Joan Wallach Scott's *Gender and the Politics of History*
Mary Wollstonecraft's *A Vindication of the Rights of Women*
Virginia Woolf's *A Room of One's Own*

GEOGRAPHY

The Brundtland Report's *Our Common Future*
Rachel Carson's *Silent Spring*
Charles Darwin's *On the Origin of Species*
James Ferguson's *The Anti-Politics Machine*
Jane Jacobs's *The Death and Life of Great American Cities*
James Lovelock's *Gaia: A New Look at Life on Earth*
Amartya Sen's *Development as Freedom*
Mathis Wackernagel & William Rees's *Our Ecological Footprint*

HISTORY

Janet Abu-Lughod's *Before European Hegemony*
Benedict Anderson's *Imagined Communities*
Bernard Bailyn's *The Ideological Origins of the American Revolution*
Hanna Batatu's *The Old Social Classes And The Revolutionary Movements Of Iraq*
Christopher Browning's *Ordinary Men: Reserve Police Batallion 101 and the Final Solution in Poland*
Edmund Burke's *Reflections on the Revolution in France*
William Cronon's *Nature's Metropolis: Chicago And The Great West*
Alfred W. Crosby's *The Columbian Exchange*
Hamid Dabashi's *Iran: A People Interrupted*
David Brion Davis's *The Problem of Slavery in the Age of Revolution*
Nathalie Zemon Davis's *The Return of Martin Guerre*
Jared Diamond's *Guns, Germs & Steel: the Fate of Human Societies*
Frank Dikotter's *Mao's Great Famine*
John W Dower's *War Without Mercy: Race And Power In The Pacific War*
W. E. B. Du Bois's *The Souls of Black Folk*
Richard J. Evans's *In Defence of History*
Lucien Febvre's *The Problem of Unbelief in the 16th Century*
Sheila Fitzpatrick's *Everyday Stalinism*

Eric Foner's *Reconstruction: America's Unfinished Revolution, 1863-1877*
Michel Foucault's *Discipline and Punish*
Michel Foucault's *History of Sexuality*
Francis Fukuyama's *The End of History and the Last Man*
John Lewis Gaddis's *We Now Know: Rethinking Cold War History*
Ernest Gellner's *Nations and Nationalism*
Eugene Genovese's *Roll, Jordan, Roll: The World the Slaves Made*
Carlo Ginzburg's *The Night Battles*
Daniel Goldhagen's *Hitler's Willing Executioners*
Jack Goldstone's *Revolution and Rebellion in the Early Modern World*
Antonio Gramsci's *The Prison Notebooks*
Alexander Hamilton, John Jay & James Madison's *The Federalist Papers*
Christopher Hill's *The World Turned Upside Down*
Carole Hillenbrand's *The Crusades: Islamic Perspectives*
Thomas Hobbes's *Leviathan*
Eric Hobsbawm's *The Age Of Revolution*
John A. Hobson's *Imperialism: A Study*
Albert Hourani's *History of the Arab Peoples*
Samuel P. Huntington's *The Clash of Civilizations and the Remaking of World Order*
C. L. R. James's *The Black Jacobins*
Tony Judt's *Postwar: A History of Europe Since 1945*
Ernst Kantorowicz's *The King's Two Bodies: A Study in Medieval Political Theology*
Paul Kennedy's *The Rise and Fall of the Great Powers*
Ian Kershaw's *The "Hitler Myth": Image and Reality in the Third Reich*
John Maynard Keynes's *The General Theory of Employment, Interest and Money*
Charles P. Kindleberger's *Manias, Panics and Crashes*
Martin Luther King Jr's *Why We Can't Wait*
Henry Kissinger's *World Order: Reflections on the Character of Nations and the Course of History*
Thomas Kuhn's *The Structure of Scientific Revolutions*
Georges Lefebvre's *The Coming of the French Revolution*
John Locke's *Two Treatises of Government*
Niccolò Machiavelli's *The Prince*
Thomas Robert Malthus's *An Essay on the Principle of Population*
Mahmood Mamdani's *Citizen and Subject: Contemporary Africa And The Legacy Of Late Colonialism*
Karl Marx's *Capital*
Stanley Milgram's *Obedience to Authority*
John Stuart Mill's *On Liberty*
Thomas Paine's *Common Sense*
Thomas Paine's *Rights of Man*
Geoffrey Parker's *Global Crisis: War, Climate Change and Catastrophe in the Seventeenth Century*
Jonathan Riley-Smith's *The First Crusade and the Idea of Crusading*
Jean-Jacques Rousseau's *The Social Contract*
Joan Wallach Scott's *Gender and the Politics of History*
Theda Skocpol's *States and Social Revolutions*
Adam Smith's *The Wealth of Nations*
Timothy Snyder's *Bloodlands: Europe Between Hitler and Stalin*
Sun Tzu's *The Art of War*
Keith Thomas's *Religion and the Decline of Magic*
Thucydides's *The History of the Peloponnesian War*
Frederick Jackson Turner's *The Significance of the Frontier in American History*
Odd Arne Westad's *The Global Cold War: Third World Interventions And The Making Of Our Times*

LITERATURE

Chinua Achebe's *An Image of Africa: Racism in Conrad's Heart of Darkness*
Roland Barthes's *Mythologies*
Homi K. Bhabha's *The Location of Culture*
Judith Butler's *Gender Trouble*
Simone De Beauvoir's *The Second Sex*
Ferdinand De Saussure's *Course in General Linguistics*
T. S. Eliot's *The Sacred Wood: Essays on Poetry and Criticism*
Zora Neale Huston's *Characteristics of Negro Expression*
Toni Morrison's *Playing in the Dark: Whiteness in the American Literary Imagination*
Edward Said's *Orientalism*
Gayatri Chakravorty Spivak's *Can the Subaltern Speak?*
Mary Wollstonecraft's *A Vindication of the Rights of Women*
Virginia Woolf's *A Room of One's Own*

PHILOSOPHY

Elizabeth Anscombe's *Modern Moral Philosophy*
Hannah Arendt's *The Human Condition*
Aristotle's *Metaphysics*
Aristotle's *Nicomachean Ethics*
Edmund Gettier's *Is Justified True Belief Knowledge?*
Georg Wilhelm Friedrich Hegel's *Phenomenology of Spirit*
David Hume's *Dialogues Concerning Natural Religion*
David Hume's *The Enquiry for Human Understanding*
Immanuel Kant's *Religion within the Boundaries of Mere Reason*
Immanuel Kant's *Critique of Pure Reason*
Søren Kierkegaard's *The Sickness Unto Death*
Søren Kierkegaard's *Fear and Trembling*
C. S. Lewis's *The Abolition of Man*
Alasdair MacIntyre's *After Virtue*
Marcus Aurelius's *Meditations*
Friedrich Nietzsche's *On the Genealogy of Morality*
Friedrich Nietzsche's *Beyond Good and Evil*
Plato's *Republic*
Plato's *Symposium*
Jean-Jacques Rousseau's *The Social Contract*
Gilbert Ryle's *The Concept of Mind*
Baruch Spinoza's *Ethics*
Sun Tzu's *The Art of War*
Ludwig Wittgenstein's *Philosophical Investigations*

POLITICS

Benedict Anderson's *Imagined Communities*
Aristotle's *Politics*
Bernard Bailyn's *The Ideological Origins of the American Revolution*
Edmund Burke's *Reflections on the Revolution in France*
John C. Calhoun's *A Disquisition on Government*
Ha-Joon Chang's *Kicking Away the Ladder*
Hamid Dabashi's *Iran: A People Interrupted*
Hamid Dabashi's *Theology of Discontent: The Ideological Foundation of the Islamic Revolution in Iran*
Robert Dahl's *Democracy and its Critics*
Robert Dahl's *Who Governs?*
David Brion Davis's *The Problem of Slavery in the Age of Revolution*

Alexis De Tocqueville's *Democracy in America*
James Ferguson's *The Anti-Politics Machine*
Frank Dikotter's *Mao's Great Famine*
Sheila Fitzpatrick's *Everyday Stalinism*
Eric Foner's *Reconstruction: America's Unfinished Revolution, 1863-1877*
Milton Friedman's *Capitalism and Freedom*
Francis Fukuyama's *The End of History and the Last Man*
John Lewis Gaddis's *We Now Know: Rethinking Cold War History*
Ernest Gellner's *Nations and Nationalism*
David Graeber's *Debt: the First 5000 Years*
Antonio Gramsci's *The Prison Notebooks*
Alexander Hamilton, John Jay & James Madison's *The Federalist Papers*
Friedrich Hayek's *The Road to Serfdom*
Christopher Hill's *The World Turned Upside Down*
Thomas Hobbes's *Leviathan*
John A. Hobson's *Imperialism: A Study*
Samuel P. Huntington's *The Clash of Civilizations and the Remaking of World Order*
Tony Judt's *Postwar: A History of Europe Since 1945*
David C. Kang's *China Rising: Peace, Power and Order in East Asia*
Paul Kennedy's *The Rise and Fall of Great Powers*
Robert Keohane's *After Hegemony*
Martin Luther King Jr.'s *Why We Can't Wait*
Henry Kissinger's *World Order: Reflections on the Character of Nations and the Course of History*
John Locke's *Two Treatises of Government*
Niccolò Machiavelli's *The Prince*
Thomas Robert Malthus's *An Essay on the Principle of Population*
Mahmood Mamdani's *Citizen and Subject: Contemporary Africa And The Legacy Of Late Colonialism*
Karl Marx's *Capital*
John Stuart Mill's *On Liberty*
John Stuart Mill's *Utilitarianism*
Hans Morgenthau's *Politics Among Nations*
Thomas Paine's *Common Sense*
Thomas Paine's *Rights of Man*
Thomas Piketty's *Capital in the Twenty-First Century*
Robert D. Putman's *Bowling Alone*
John Rawls's *Theory of Justice*
Jean-Jacques Rousseau's *The Social Contract*
Theda Skocpol's *States and Social Revolutions*
Adam Smith's *The Wealth of Nations*
Sun Tzu's *The Art of War*
Henry David Thoreau's *Civil Disobedience*
Thucydides's *The History of the Peloponnesian War*
Kenneth Waltz's *Theory of International Politics*
Max Weber's *Politics as a Vocation*
Odd Arne Westad's *The Global Cold War: Third World Interventions And The Making Of Our Times*

POSTCOLONIAL STUDIES

Roland Barthes's *Mythologies*
Frantz Fanon's *Black Skin, White Masks*
Homi K. Bhabha's *The Location of Culture*
Gustavo Gutiérrez's *A Theology of Liberation*
Edward Said's *Orientalism*
Gayatri Chakravorty Spivak's *Can the Subaltern Speak?*

PSYCHOLOGY

Gordon Allport's *The Nature of Prejudice*
Alan Baddeley & Graham Hitch's *Aggression: A Social Learning Analysis*
Albert Bandura's *Aggression: A Social Learning Analysis*
Leon Festinger's *A Theory of Cognitive Dissonance*
Sigmund Freud's *The Interpretation of Dreams*
Betty Friedan's *The Feminine Mystique*
Michael R. Gottfredson & Travis Hirschi's *A General Theory of Crime*
Eric Hoffer's *The True Believer: Thoughts on the Nature of Mass Movements*
William James's *Principles of Psychology*
Elizabeth Loftus's *Eyewitness Testimony*
A. H. Maslow's *A Theory of Human Motivation*
Stanley Milgram's *Obedience to Authority*
Steven Pinker's *The Better Angels of Our Nature*
Oliver Sacks's *The Man Who Mistook His Wife For a Hat*
Richard Thaler & Cass Sunstein's *Nudge: Improving Decisions About Health, Wealth and Happiness*
Amos Tversky's *Judgment under Uncertainty: Heuristics and Biases*
Philip Zimbardo's *The Lucifer Effect*

SCIENCE

Rachel Carson's *Silent Spring*
William Cronon's *Nature's Metropolis: Chicago And The Great West*
Alfred W. Crosby's *The Columbian Exchange*
Charles Darwin's *On the Origin of Species*
Richard Dawkin's *The Selfish Gene*
Thomas Kuhn's *The Structure of Scientific Revolutions*
Geoffrey Parker's *Global Crisis: War, Climate Change and Catastrophe in the Seventeenth Century*
Mathis Wackernagel & William Rees's *Our Ecological Footprint*

SOCIOLOGY

Michelle Alexander's *The New Jim Crow: Mass Incarceration in the Age of Colorblindness*
Gordon Allport's *The Nature of Prejudice*
Albert Bandura's *Aggression: A Social Learning Analysis*
Hanna Batatu's *The Old Social Classes And The Revolutionary Movements Of Iraq*
Ha-Joon Chang's *Kicking Away the Ladder*
W. E. B. Du Bois's *The Souls of Black Folk*
Émile Durkheim's *On Suicide*
Frantz Fanon's *Black Skin, White Masks*
Frantz Fanon's *The Wretched of the Earth*
Eric Foner's *Reconstruction: America's Unfinished Revolution, 1863-1877*
Eugene Genovese's *Roll, Jordan, Roll: The World the Slaves Made*
Jack Goldstone's *Revolution and Rebellion in the Early Modern World*
Antonio Gramsci's *The Prison Notebooks*
Richard Herrnstein & Charles A Murray's *The Bell Curve: Intelligence and Class Structure in American Life*
Eric Hoffer's *The True Believer: Thoughts on the Nature of Mass Movements*
Jane Jacobs's *The Death and Life of Great American Cities*
Robert Lucas's *Why Doesn't Capital Flow from Rich to Poor Countries?*
Jay Macleod's *Ain't No Makin' It: Aspirations and Attainment in a Low Income Neighborhood*
Elaine May's *Homeward Bound: American Families in the Cold War Era*
Douglas McGregor's *The Human Side of Enterprise*
C. Wright Mills's *The Sociological Imagination*

Thomas Piketty's *Capital in the Twenty-First Century*
Robert D. Putman's *Bowling Alone*
David Riesman's *The Lonely Crowd: A Study of the Changing American Character*
Edward Said's *Orientalism*
Joan Wallach Scott's *Gender and the Politics of History*
Theda Skocpol's *States and Social Revolutions*
Max Weber's *The Protestant Ethic and the Spirit of Capitalism*

THEOLOGY

Augustine's *Confessions*
Benedict's *Rule of St Benedict*
Gustavo Gutiérrez's *A Theology of Liberation*
Carole Hillenbrand's *The Crusades: Islamic Perspectives*
David Hume's *Dialogues Concerning Natural Religion*
Immanuel Kant's *Religion within the Boundaries of Mere Reason*
Ernst Kantorowicz's *The King's Two Bodies: A Study in Medieval Political Theology*
Søren Kierkegaard's *The Sickness Unto Death*
C. S. Lewis's *The Abolition of Man*
Saba Mahmood's *The Politics of Piety: The Islamic Revival and the Feminist Subject*
Baruch Spinoza's *Ethics*
Keith Thomas's *Religion and the Decline of Magic*

COMING SOON

Chris Argyris's *The Individual and the Organisation*
Seyla Benhabib's *The Rights of Others*
Walter Benjamin's *The Work Of Art in the Age of Mechanical Reproduction*
John Berger's *Ways of Seeing*
Pierre Bourdieu's *Outline of a Theory of Practice*
Mary Douglas's *Purity and Danger*
Roland Dworkin's *Taking Rights Seriously*
James G. March's *Exploration and Exploitation in Organisational Learning*
Ikujiro Nonaka's *A Dynamic Theory of Organizational Knowledge Creation*
Griselda Pollock's *Vision and Difference*
Amartya Sen's *Inequality Re-Examined*
Susan Sontag's *On Photography*
Yasser Tabbaa's *The Transformation of Islamic Art*
Ludwig von Mises's *Theory of Money and Credit*